Woodside, Pear Tree Grove P.O.

The emancipation monument at Woodside, St Mary (photo by Velma Pollard). The Akan symbol *Gye Nyame*, representing the omnipotence and omnipresence of God, was chosen by the community. The monument was designed by Kay Hamilton Anderson, former head of the art department at the Edna Manley School of the Visual and Performing Arts and a descendent of Africans enslaved in the greater Woodside area.

Woodside, Pear Tree Grove P.O.

Erna Brodber

University of the West Indies Press
Jamaica • Barbados • Trinidad and Tobago

University of the West Indies Press
1A Aqueduct Flats   Mona
Kingston 7   Jamaica
www.uwipress.com

08 07 06 05 04   5 4 3 2 1

CATALOGUING IN PUBLICATION DATA

Brodber, Erna
Woodside, Pear Tree Grove P.O. / Erna Brodber
p. cm.
Includes bibliographical references.

ISBN: 976-640-152-7

1. Woodside (Jamaica) – History. 2. Villages – Jamaica – St Mary –
History. 3. Peasantry – Jamaica – Woodside – History. 4. Whites –
Jamaica – Woodside – History. 5. Woodside (Jamaica) – Social conditions.
I. Title.

F1891.S2 B76 2004   972.9704

Cover photo: Woodside Road, by Shawn Fong (?)
Book and cover design by Robert Harris.
Set in Sabon 10.5/14 x 24.
Printed in Canada.

Contents

Preface

I was born in 1940 in Woodside in the parish of St Mary in the island of Jamaica. In recent years the post office that serves Woodside, though the building remains in St Mary, has been administratively moved to St Catherine; thus my current address is Woodside, Pear Tree Grove P.O., St Mary/St Catherine, Jamaica, West Indies. I am the second of my parents' five children but the first to be born in Woodside. All the others were helped into this world by Euro-trained health workers; I came in with the help of the local nana, Miss Rachel, a woman who looked neither right nor left and seemed to talk to none but God. They buried my navel string under the blue bell tree, a shrub that actually produced white bell-shaped flowers.

My parents came from elsewhere to Woodside, St Mary while my mother was carrying me, but did not settle down here until 1945. My mother was a schoolteacher who worked outside of the village. She took my older sister with her. It was only when leisure and the mail van or bread van came together that Woodside and I saw them. My father's life was not very much more settled. Having bought the house and the land, there was not much left to begin a farming enterprise. He sought money outside. Today, he was a salesman of patent medicine; tomorrow, a lumber salesman. He even tried, unsuccessfully of course, to use his skills got externally from Pittman's Institute in Bath, England, to make a living as a court reporter. My mother got a job at Woodside School in 1945. Something must have happened for my father too, for his journeys out decreased.

While my parents dallied here and there, I for the most part lived in Woodside, at the mercy of servants overseen by my attentive but floating father. There was in me a deep loneliness and sadness that culminated in physical illness. The spirits of Woodside kept me company and helped me to survive. I was and am aware of this. My father's sister, the first of their clan to settle in Woodside, had come to the village as a school teacher and had very soon thereafter retired into marriage with one of the late-arriving Walkers. I was sometimes left in her household. Occasionally I was taken out of the village to stay with my maternal grandmother, whose house was closer to where my mother worked than ours was. There I yearned for the spirits of Woodside, for the place where my navel string was buried.

I lived in Woodside until age eleven, when I went to high school in Kingston. Every day of my holidays, except for a couple weeks spent in Santa Cruz, St Elizabeth in 1957, and a couple days in Portland with my uncle, and the occasional few days per year with my mother's mother, was spent in Woodside, Pear Tree Grove P.O., St Mary/St Catherine. Work and university reduced my stays. My parents moved out, one through death, in 1962. Illness, apparently difficult to diagnose, sent me back to Woodside in 1972. I was sure the spirits would cure me once more. My father took me seriously and built me a small house on the family land. I moved back for a year, later commuting between Kingston, where I worked at the University of the West Indies, and Woodside.

When the university decided that it no longer needed my teaching and research skills, I decided to practice them in my village. Out of this determination came a theory of community development that had as its central motif the giving of information concerning themselves to the people of the community. Knowledge is power and self-knowledge is greater power. I did not coin the phrase. That people should not only have knowledge of themselves but feel that others want this knowledge and should share in a two-way process with them, was part of the theory of community development ensuing out of my sojourn in my homeland. This book is born out of that understanding.

Research towards the writing of *Woodside, Pear Tree Grove P.O.* began formally at Randolph Macon College in Virginia, where I was then working, and Gettysburg College, Pennsylvania, where I had worked. Their students visited the village with me in 1993, living-in with families and helping them to write their histories. Some of the students got credits for this; others were satisfied to have only the experience of rural life. Through the family histories collected by the foreign students came the revelation of village traditions concerning the development and history of the area. Thereafter there was continual movement between oral and archaeological sources as well as archival sources – maps, deeds and titles, registers of births, deaths and marriages, and inscriptions on tombs. There were two "give-back" sessions with villagers during which memories, verifying and debunking each other, clarified data on the village.

This final product was intended for the students of the Woodside elementary school. I know that they cannot by themselves access this gift and I rely now on their teachers to pass the knowledge on to them. This work is so written that it stretches its readers to seek further information on issues pertinent to Jamaicans. The hope is that it will be the beginning of self-inquiry into the connection between Jamaica, the villages in and families of Jamaica, and the various other places from which Jamaicans were brought to live and work here. It is also hoped that the many people from Woodside who have left the area will read this, that memories will flood back and that they will be moved to creative use of the vast acreages of land which they have left to the mosquitoes and the grass lice, ticks and the very dangerous duck ants.

Woodside, Pear Tree Grove P.O., one of the first histories of a village in Jamaica, will be of relevance to students of community development and of the history of Jamaica. It has tried to present the history of the underclass – the enslaved and indentured workers – in interaction with their social and physical environment, and in such a way that the man in the street may see a portrait of himself and of his forefathers. This product is presented with several questions raised and left unanswered. To this extent, it is a work-in-progress. The hope is that its readers, some of whom we know must have the answers, will feel moved to write their own version for public consumption.

Erna Brodber
Woodside
Pear Tree Grove P.O.
St Mary/St Catherine
Jamaica

Acknowledgements

Swithin Wilmot of the Department of History at the University of the West Indies, Mona, came to Woodside to give a lecture. His topic was "St Mary in the Immediate Post-Emancipation Period". He spoke to an audience of grandmothers and grandfathers, some young adults and some children, a tiny proportion of whom had had more than primary school education or were actually in secondary school. His audience was transfixed. One grandmother asked, "Why didn't they tell us these things before?" Another who lived three miles away, offered a lift home before the end of the talk, responded, "When my history is being discussed, I don't move." A visiting academic from Yale University, seeing the size and make-up of the audience, commented that to have such an audience in rapt attention had to be the high point of Swithin's career as a lecturer. He was jealous and so was I. As a result, I decided to go out and find information to add to what Swithin had given. Woodside is a small part of St Mary. If I could give his audience information which focused solely on their forbears who had lived in Woodside, I argued, they would appreciate my efforts even more than Swithin's. Research on the history of Woodside began.

My research findings were intended to be transmitted, like Swithin's presentation, orally. Sharon Chacko, batik artist and historian, was at the first of these oral presentations. She declared that she couldn't wait to read the book: she had assumed that what she was hearing was the first chapter of a work being prepared for publication. Velma Pollard, an educator and my sister, required by me to share my excitement at finding the 1828 will of Dr William John Neilson, the nineteenth-century owner of Woodside Estate, was shocked that such finds and this excitement were not meant to be laid down for posterity. Thank you Swithin Wilmot, Sharon Chacko and Velma Pollard for forcing me to do the research and to get it into print.

To Aunt Leah, Mass Peggy, Mass Arnold, Mass Vernie, Mass Lennie, Mass B, Mass Levi, all passed on, thank you for opening your past to me and to posterity. Miss Pearl, Mass Roy, Mass Bishie, Massa Boy, Mass Keith, Mass Ranny, Mass Ron, Miss Vie, Aunt Es and the very many still with us, who gave me information, I am glad that you will be able to read what I have done with your family histories. The mistakes, of course, are mine; I hope that they are few.

To the ten students of Gettysburg College who, with their advisor Bob Frederickson, came to live with and to collect histories from a select group of Woodside families, thank you for your help in the field. To Mario Palmer (Tony), thanks for your help in the archives, and to the staff of the National Library of Jamaica, in particular, thank you for the beautiful space in which I spent many happy hours at work. To my nephew Michael Pollard and my brother Owen Brodber, thanks for the variety of discarded computers that you kindly made available to me to continue with this work.

Many thanks to Martin Mordecai for coming to my home and photographing a map that would disintegrate if shifted from its place on the wall; to Velma Pollard, who battled the bushes to photograph "One Bubby Susan"; to my mother (deceased), whose passion for keeping scrapbooks presented me with useful data; to Linda Speth, who was sure this work ought to be published and to Shivaun Hearne, who guided the process. To the many who supported with kind and often unspoken words, thanks.

Introduction

Defining the Space

If we are to trace the history of the village called Woodside or any other place in Jamaica in such a way that the residents are able to locate themselves in it, we need to begin with a clear outline of the physical space to which we are alluding. Few places are today like biblical cities of old, hemmed in and defined by walls; determining the actual location and dimensions of such spaces as Woodside is difficult. Signposts can give us the definition we need, but the place called Woodside has not been known to appear on any such signposts or consistently on road maps or official survey maps of the parish of St Mary, of which it is a part. One way of proceeding with the task of locating a place when no physical signs exist to guide the search, is to let the people who say they live in the area draw its boundaries. This is the path that this history of Woodside takes.

Mr Vernal Kelly, interviewed on 12 August 1989 and born in the area in 1912, describing the physical boundaries of the place he calls Woodside, says:

> The area called Woodside embodied Rock Spring and Smailfield . . . Mongrave was one district and Woodside was the other which had Smailfield in it . . . and it came right up occupying Hopewell and back to [the place in Woodside] where they call Shadduck Tree and then it borders again down to Lee Bridge so that it occupies the whole of the hillside here they call Bramber so that the whole of this part come to the border of St Catherine. Then it takes in Dryland and occupies all that section where Mr Nelson at Rock Spring and Remekie [are] and then now you have Smailfield come back to Hopewell back to Mr McIntosh [at Stapleton].

Mr Kelly, who died in 1992, was at the time of this interview one of Woodside's oldest citizens. He was a bright mind, one of the earliest Jamaicans to enter the Hope Agricultural School; he had worked in the area as a civil servant and a farmer; he had in his private and public capacities thought about the matter of locating Woodside and describing its boundaries. He thought it fit to define Woodside as a social space, a place in which people interact with each other in the pursuit of the necessities of life, as well as a physical space.

Education and spiritual sustenance were in Mr Kelly's day very important areas of behaviour and ones in which people were involved with each other over long periods of time. Children spent seven years together in elementary school; church members spent a lifetime together. Mr Kelly

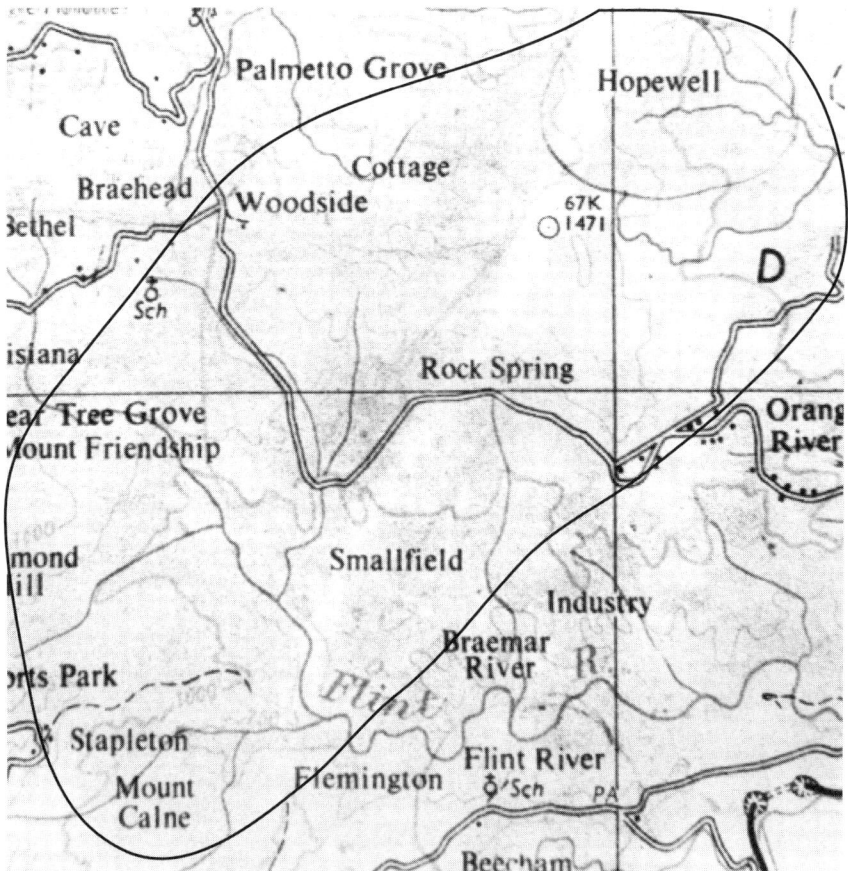

Map 1 Detail of a 1952 survey map of showing Woodside as defined by Mr Kelly (photo by Martin Mordecai)

used residence of the members of the Woodside Anglican church (St Gabriel's), and attendance at the school which then shared its building, to arrive at the boundaries of the space that interests us here. The area delineated in map 1 and extracted from one of the few survey maps on which the word "Woodside" appears, is Woodside, according to the evidence of Mr Kelly.

Mr Kelly, born in 1912, went to school in Woodside between 1919 and 1926. Was the physical space occupied by the Woodside people as they sought education from elementary school, the same in later years? This work wants to look at Woodside up to 1944. Following Mr Kelly, we use social interaction in the Woodside School, and to a lesser extent the Woodside Anglican church, to define our physical area. An examination of the school records for the years 1928–48 does show children attending school from the points Mr Kelly mentions and from other points such as Cow Pen, Cross Road, Bridge Hill, which are known to be areas within a mile of the school and which can therefore be called subsections of Woodside. There are areas further afield not mentioned in Mr Kelly's definition of the area.

Many children came to Woodside School between 1928 and 1948 from Palmetto Grove and Louisiana. There were others from Change

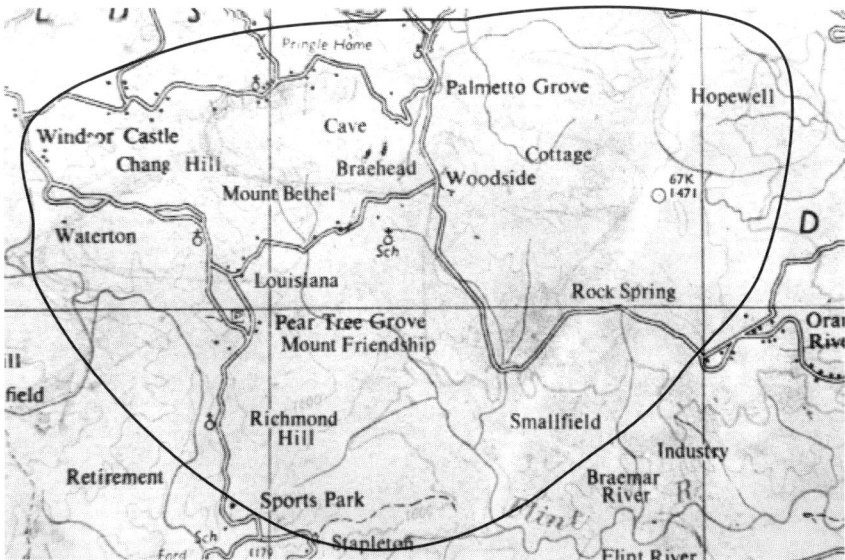

Map 2 Detail of a 1952 map showing Woodside as a school district, 1928–48 (photo by Martin Mordecai)

Hill, Brae Head, Petersfield, Rhyon Hill, Richmond Hill, Jumper, John Crow Hill, even from Windsor Castle, about four miles away. A comparison of Mr Kelly's definition of the area this school serviced in his day with attendance in this later period, indicates that the social space of the school community was extended between 1928 and 1948. This later school district is shown in map 2.

It is this definition of the boundaries of Woodside, boundaries that expanded after Mr Kelly left elementary school, and which are described in the map above, that we use in this work.

Chapter 1

Woodside

The Socio/Physical Past

The known social history of Jamaica, of which Woodside is a north-easterly district, begins with the Arawaks, now called Tainos. "One/Long Bubby Susan" (figure 1), located in that part of Woodside called Dryland, was called an Arawak carving by Frank Cundall, the island's major historian in the first decade of the twentieth century. If he is right, Tainos did live in this area, as in some other parts of Jamaica, in the days before Columbus made this island known to the people of Europe. It is less sure that the Spaniards whom Columbus's new knowledge brought to Jamaica between 1509 and 1655, did live in Woodside. There are several stories in the folk accounts, of Spanish jars buried in the area and even of Spanish spirits left to guard this treasure from everlasting to everlasting. No other evidence has so far been adduced of the Spanish presence, and as the one story in which the ghost is identified gives him the non-Spanish name, Frank, this evidence becomes shaky indeed.

Map 3, made public in 1804, gives, as maps do, the position of certain places in relation to others. This map, a part of southern St Mary and northern St Catherine, is likely to have been prepared some years before its publication and would thus report on the situation as it was before 1804. The name Woodside does not appear on this map. Apparently, the place we today call Woodside was not called so in the years preceding 1804. There are areas, however, from which Woodside students walked to school in 1919 when Mr Kelly was among them, and

Figure 1 One/Long Bubby Susan (photo by Velma Pollard)

in 1928 to 1948, the period covered by the school registers mentioned above, which are listed on this map. Most notable of them are Palmetto Grove and Hopewell. These districts, according to the map, covered relatively large acreages in the early nineteenth century. Note too the existence on this map of water courses which retain their names. See, for instance, the Rio Sambre and the Flint River. With these name retentions – Palmetto Grove, Hopewell, Rio Sambre and Flint River – we are now able to locate the place we today call Woodside because we know the current physical relationship of these places to Woodside. Woodside is thus the area encircled on the map.

When you look closely at this map, you will see that the words written on it are in several kinds of type. There are, for instance, words in bold type. The names which fall outside of the circle on the map and which are in this type are Tremolesworth, Pembroke Hall, Crawle Pond, Hermon Hill, Donnington Castle and Hazard. These names, we know from prior research, designate large sugar plantations. The only such words within the circle are Palmetto Grove and Hopewell; we can conclude, then, that these are the only parts of Woodside that were sugar plantation areas.

Look closer and you will see another kind of type. Look, for instance, close to the name Palmetto Grove and you will see to its left, the words "W Neilson's". There are many such possessives on the edge of, within and outside of the circle – McKay's, Wright's, Forbes's, Page's, Facey's, Grant's, Jordan's, Buchanan's, Capelton's, Shryer's. Within the circle are Grant's, Forbes's, Harrison and Hart's, Parker's, Neilson's, Burrowes's, Turner's, Cunningham's, Benwell's, Pollock's. Obviously, areas indicated in this type belonged to the people mentioned but were either not yet given special names or were not significant enough at the time to be entered on the map.

The existence of certain tombstones in the area, and their inscriptions, indicate that some of the names mentioned on the map of 1804 belonged to people who were indeed residents of the area. This source helps us to put current place names on the old map. Found on the property of Mr Moses James at Smailfield is the following dedication:

> Sacred to the memory of William Turner for many years a respectable inhabitant of the parish of St Mary, Jamaica and as he lived respected so he died regretted. He departed this life November 26th 1801 age 45 years. As a memento of affectionate regard for the best of husbands, this tablet is erected

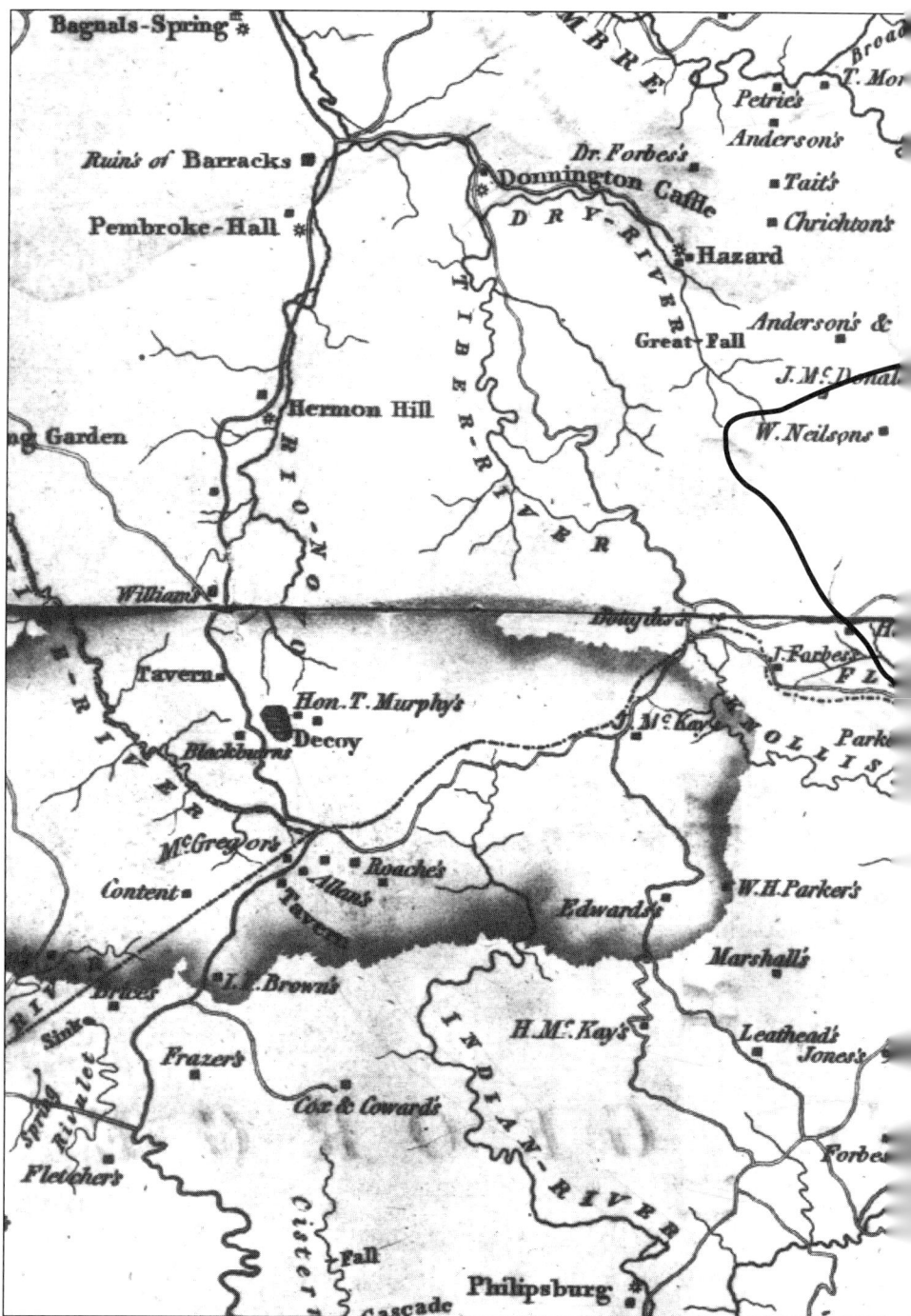

Map 3 Detail from the 1804 map of St Mary by Robertson (National Library of Jamaica)

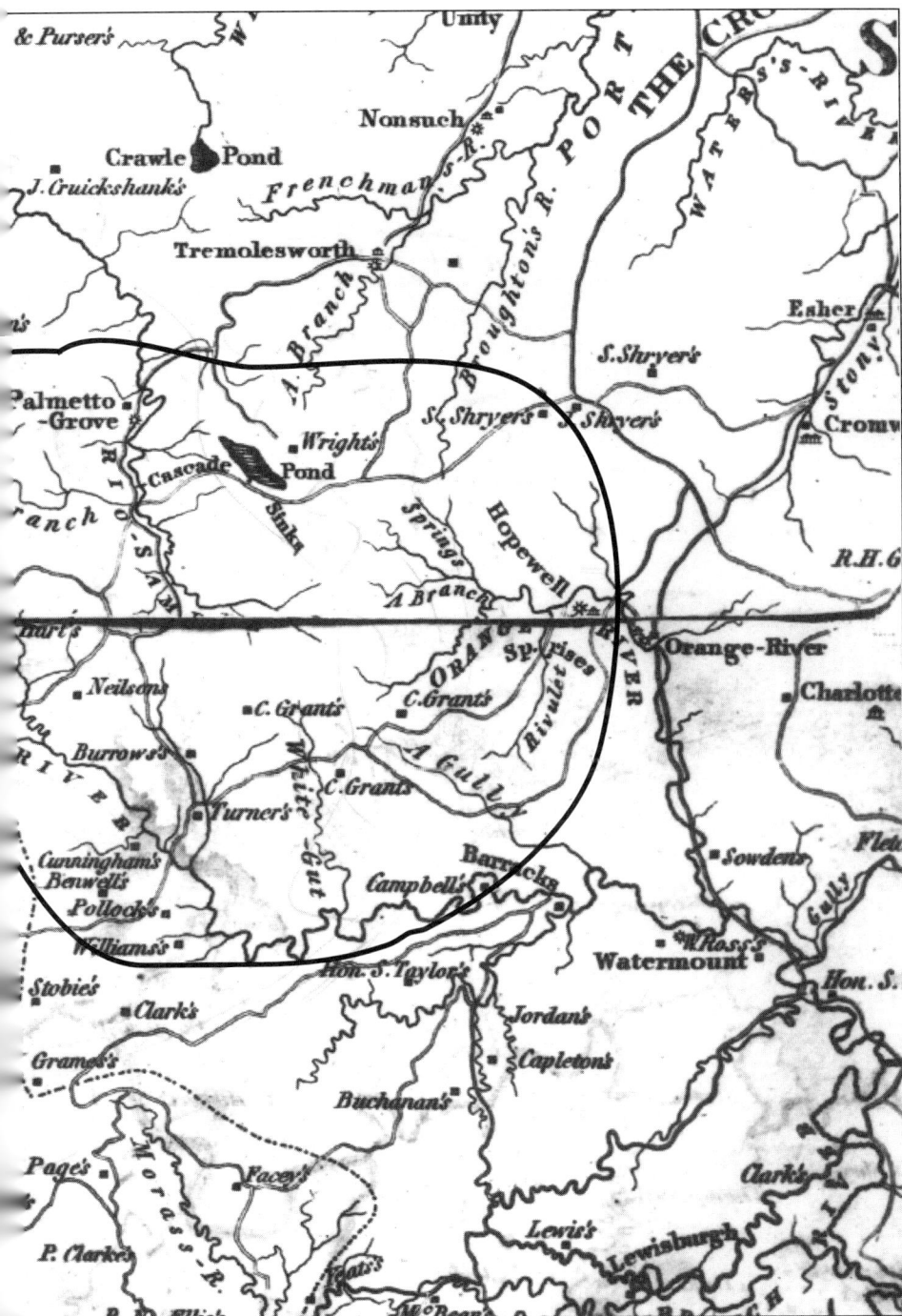

& Purser's

Unity

Nonsuch

Crawle Pond

J. Cruickshank's

Frenchman's R.

Broughton's R.

THE CR

PORT

WATERS'S-RIVER

Tremolesworth

Esher

S. Shryer's

Stony

Palmetto
-Grove

A Branch

St. Shryer's

S. Shryer's

Cromv

Wright's

Cascade
Pond

Rio-Sam

Sinks

Springs

A Branch

Hopewell

R.H.G

Hart's

ORANGE

RIVER

Sp-rises

Orange-River

Neilson's

C. Grant's

C. Grant's

Rivulet

Charlotte

RIVER

Burrow's

C. Grants

A Gully

White Gut

Turner's

Sowden's

Fle

Cunningham's
Benwell's

Campbell's

Barracks

W.Ross?

Gully

Pollock's

Hon. S. Taylor's

Watermount

Hon. S.

Williams's

Stobie's

Clark's

Jordan's

Grame's

Capleton's

Buchanan's

Page's

Morass. R.

Facey's

Clark's

P. Clarke's

Lewis's

Lewisburgh

R D Ellis's

McBean's

by the desire of Mrs Jane Turner also to the memory of William Turner infant son of the above William and Jane Turner who departed this life November 26th 1801, aged 5.

This is clearly the Turner of Turner's on the 1804 map. Evidently Turner lived in the Woodside area in 1801 with his family, and died on the same day as his infant son. We can now put the name Smailfield alongside the words Turner's on the circle on the 1804 map.

We can do something similar with the Burrowes's on the map. A 1994 search of a field across the road and across the stream facing the Seventh Day Church of God – Mrs Lillian Edwards's church – at Rock Spring unearthed a tomb with the following dedication:

In memory of Edward Marchant Burrowes who died the 10th of January 1812 aged 31. This excellent youngman has left few to trouble him. One superior, the remembrance of his extreme worth will ever be treasured in the heart of his surviving sister. In gratitude for his never-ending kindness is offered this slight tribute to his beloved and bereaved memory.

This young man, a resident of Rock Spring, a part of the area that the Woodside School served in the early twentieth century, was at most twenty-three years old when the 1804 map was published. His death was regretted not by a wife or by parents but by a sister. Were they pre-deceased by their parents? Within the oral tradition lies the story that the Burrowes who owned the property had planted two Mary Gould mango trees at the entrance to his house. These trees were brought as plants from England; they still exist today. Was it this young man who brought these trees from England and planted them in Rock Spring?

There is still another tombstone in the area. It lies in the Woodside Anglican churchyard. This one reads: "Here lies the body of John Neilson Esq. who departed this life XXVth June MDCCC aged LXI years. His widow Frances Maidstone Neilson has erected this marble [indeci-pherable] mournful testimony of her affection and regret." We can safely put Woodside property beside the word Neilson's within the circle on the 1804 map.

When Cromwell's men came to the Caribbean in 1655, it was not to capture Jamaica from the Spanish, as they did do, but to take Santo Domingo. What to make of this "second prize", which did not have the deposits of precious stones that they had sought? One alternative thought of and used by the British government, was the Barbados model – to lease the island to influential men called proprietors on condition that they see to its development, and out of this development let them contribute by way of trade and taxes to the revenues of the Crown. These proprietors were given patents by the British government, that is, according to the Oxford dictionary, the "sole right to use" an article.

The article in this case was the area served in the early twentieth century by the Woodside elementary school, which we shall now call the Woodside school area. These proprietors acted like contractors – they encouraged others to settle the island under their protection and with their financial support, giving them also patents to use portions of their patented lands. One of the proprietors controlling the Woodside school area, according to the maps found in the collection at the National Library of Jamaica, was Lord Bathurst. He was granted, on 9 June 1674, four thousand acres of those lands through which the Knollis and the Flint Rivers run.[1]

Another name associated with large proprietorship in the greater Woodside area was that of the Parkers. They controlled the Palmetto Grove/Louisiana area and were in dispute in 1784 concerning ownership of some lands between the Rio Sambre and the Flint River, handed down from Bathurst to the Grants.[2] The Parkers must have prevailed, for a map of 1785,[3] referring to the intended sale of Smailfield, part of that area, describes it as land originally owned by John Parker and subcontracted to others for development. Names associated with the subcontract in this part of the Woodside school area are Oaxley Andrews and Simmond Hammond. They eventually sold these lands, the profits presumably going to subcontractor, contractor and the British government. The purchasers were William Turner of today's Smailfield, William Burrowes of today's Rock Spring, and Alexander Cummings and Messrs Watson and Hamilton of what looks like today's Stapleton. One subcontractor west of the Flint River, under the Parker patent, was William Rushley. It is out of his 750 acres that the Burnetts in 1777 got five acres and one rood to begin what was to be Louisiana.[4] Neighbouring subcontractors, as we see from the same document, were Michael Bergh, Dr Thomas Traphan and Stephen Vidad, names that seem other than English. Neilson's Woodside property comes out of these subcontracts.

Another name associated with the Woodside school area in its eighteenth-century days was that of Alexander Wright. Wright controlled

Palmetto Grove, formerly part of the Parker patent,[5] and until 1793 that hundred-acre plot beginning at the gate of the Woodside plantation house, bounded by the road passing Petersfield to Palmetto Grove on one side and on the other a by "rivulet running into the Rio Sambre".[6] This land is what is today's John Crow Hill–Jumper area. Wright could not pay his mortgage and this portion of land was alienated to William Peterswold, through whom it was eventually incorporated into Woodside proper in 1819. Wright's Palmetto Grove was in sugar and cattle. It is entirely possible that this part of Woodside was similarly engaged. Kofi Agorsah, an archaeologist formerly attached to the Department of History of the University of the West Indies, dates some ruins near to today's Woodside School as mid-eighteenth century. It could be that the subcontractors with the un-English names had not only held the lands but had lived here and had developed them as sugar holdings.

It could be also that John Neilson had been here since the mid-eighteenth century and had himself developed these lands. The records available to us do not say when John Neilson bought his lands. We can assume, however, that he was actively in production here in 1798 for his wife, Frances Maidstone Neilson, sold a slave in that year.[7] In addition, at the time of his death in 1800, Neilson had pastures, feeding troughs and buildings on his property. These must have taken him a considerable time to put in place.[8] That he was buried here indicates that he quite likely did live here.

A re-visit to the map of 1804 shows that there are small black blocks beside some names and not beside others. There are blocks beside the names of those whom we know were buried there. There is also one beside the name Parker. We can infer from this that William Parker, who owned lands in the Woodside school area, today called Louisiana and who was the 1798 purchaser of Mrs Neilson's slave, also lived in the area.

The map collection at the National Library of Jamaica helps us to put shapes and sizes to these places. An undated reference tells us that thirty-five acres of land, patented by Mary Parker and formerly patented by Louis Fortune, is "bounded north-easterly on Hazard Estate, west by Change Hill Plantation and on the remaining land belonging to John Neilson".[9] We know that this map refers to a time before 1804 since there is no mention of Louis Fortune or Mary Parker on our 1804 map. "Remaining land belonging to John Neilson . . .": the indication from this datum is that John Neilson had lands near to the Change Hill

Figure 2 Woodside Estate gate leading to Dr Neilson's great house, *c.*1952 (photo by Lester Murray)

Plantation and Hazard Estate before 1804, and perhaps in an earlier time had more land in that area. This land would have abutted "W. Neilson's". A deed tells us among other things that John Neilson had, in 1801, a thirty-acre plot "bounding north on Carron Hall, east on Palmetto Grove, west on Harrison and Hart and south on the remaining part of the same land".[10] This is the location of the piece of land owned by John Neilson that is mentioned in the reference to Mary Parker. With this information we can definitely conclude that at his death in 1800 John Neilson had land near to Change Hill and to Carron Hall, which might have been part of a larger acreage of land from which some was sold prior to 1800.

This same deed also refers to another Neilson location. We are told that John Neilson has two pieces of land, one of twenty acres and another of forty acres, "being part of a 500 acre plot patented by Francis Grossier, bounded easterly on the road leading from Spanish Town to St Mary, south in the possession of Patience Hermit and north-westerly on the partition line of John and William Parker". This looks like the area on the 1804 map that is close to the bend in the Knollis River and which today we call the Louisiana/Richmond Hill/Pear Tree Grove area.

Another map dated 1806 tells us that in or about 1806, fifty-one of the 148 acres of Waterton, the property of "Mr Jon [Jonathan] Forbes" was "(i)n coffee by Mr Neilson".[11] Are these two pieces of land the same? It appears so. Neilson's property, by 1806, seems to share a boundary with Waterton. That this part of his property is found on a diagram of Waterton leads to questions of tenure: Was this piece of land in his possession by rent, lease or purchase?

Another map found in the National Library of Jamaica discusses a change of property between a Neilson, Dr William John Neilson, and James Dean(s) in 1819.[12] The lands exchanged are the part of Woodside near to Palmetto Grove, and the part of Palmetto Grove nearest to Hopewell. They were twenty-four-acre plots. That piece close to Hopewell went to Neilson and the piece close to Palmetto Grove, very likely the one close to Carron Hall and Change Hill, went to Dean. The new Neilson land, in today's terms, would be between John Crow Hill and Hopewell. Another undated map[13] shows Rock Spring's one hundred acres, with a top piece of thirty acres. This top piece abuts Woodside. These data make the Neilson's Woodside, at some time in the early nineteenth century, an area that spread from Waterton in the west to Rock Spring and Hopewell in the east, from the Knollis River to the Rio Sambre. A map reference to Smailfield[14] of 1839 makes Woodside a northern boundary of that plantation. By these data the Woodside estate in the early nineteenth century stretched southward from Change Hill and Petersfield to Smailfield. Woodside's north to south and east to west acreage was clearly far in excess of the 148 acres of Forbes's Waterton, the 190 of the Turner's Smailfield in 1806 and the 328 under new ownership, and the 130 acres of the Rock Spring plantation.

The Neilson's Woodside would have been one of the leading plantations in the area, and the Neilsons, the leading or one of the leading families in the area. John Neilson died in 1800, a year before William Turner. Funereal style could not have changed over so short a period, but Neilson was remembered in roman figures and in polished marble and Turner in unpolished marble and ordinary numerals. This disparity is possibly a mark of the relative prosperity and status of the two. Since the school that attracted the early-twentieth-century residents of the Woodside area was, between 1928 and 1948, situated within yards of Neilson's tomb, the spot on which it is built would have been part of the old Woodside plantation. Oral sources attest to this. The foregoing establishes, historically, a social and economic distinction between Woodside and the areas adjacent to it.

Accepting the status of the Neilsons and of their property to have been higher than that of most of their neighbours, we shall now distinguish the areas serviced by the Woodside School and that which is the universe of this study, into "Woodside proper" and "greater Woodside". We call the area that the Neilson property covered Woodside proper, and the rest of the area including this, as mentioned in Mr Kelly's report and as identified in the school registers, the greater Woodside area.

From works of the geographer/historian, Barry Higman, we learn that the area outside of the circle marked "Hon. S. Taylor's" was Flint River Pen;[15] it is today called Flint River. In 1804 it was owned by Simon Taylor, born in 1740; he died in 1813. Simon Taylor, for many years a member of the House of Legislature, was a Jamaican-born attorney who made himself the wealthiest resident of the island out of the work he did for absentee planters.[16] He had property in several other parts of Jamaica and in other areas of the parish of St Mary, one of the latter being Montrose Pen. This holding was, during his lifetime, at the junction of the Flint River and the Sue River. Here he dealt in cattle, which in one form or another supplied other nearby estates; among these was Hopewell, one of the areas served in the early twentieth century by the Woodside School. We know from other sources that a Charles Grant did own Hopewell Estate, and he was one of the two members of the House of Assembly for St Mary, a barrister, and custos of St Mary between 1807 and 1817.[17] If Charles is the "C. Grant" on the 1804 map, then he owned not only Hopewell Estate but also its immediate environs.

Following the Flint River, a part of which defined Simon Taylor's property, leads us to putting another place name alongside a family name. According to the 1804 map, Forbes owns property at the head of the Flint River. Oral sources and the maps discussed above help to identify this place as today's Waterton, an area in the vicinity of Change Hill, Petersfield, Windsor Castle and Louisiana, all places from which children came to learn at the Woodside School in the early days of this century. An 1806 map[18] confirms its location to have been as it is today, south of Change Hill and Windsor Castle. The identification of Waterton makes it possible for us to put the current names Brae Head, Blue Gate and Change Hill beside the words "Harrison and Hart's" on the 1804 map. Completing this part of the jigsaw puzzle allows us an intelligent

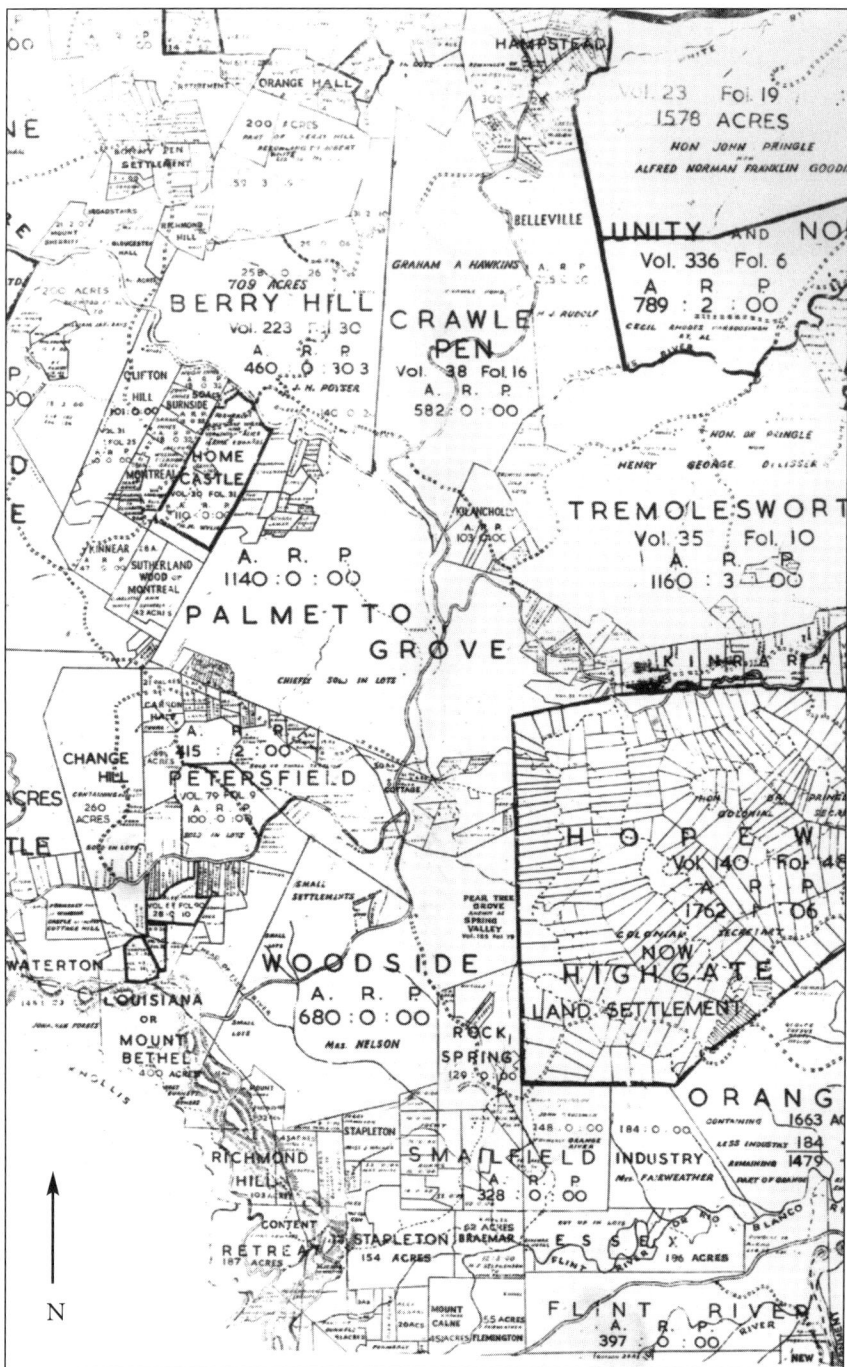

Map 4 Map of the Woodside area, 1880 (National Library of Jamaica)

guess concerning the location of Stapleton. It must be that area south of Smailfield that on the 1806 map of that area is marked Pollock's, and which on the 1804 map is in the vicinity represented by the words "Cunningham's", "Benwell's" and "Pollock's".

Rock Spring, Woodside proper, Smailfield, Stapleton and Louisiana were coffee-growing areas, and Palmetto Grove was a sugar plantation in the nineteenth century, according to an official document called "Appendix to the seventh report from the select committee on sugar and coffee planting".[19] This document is part of a parliamentary report to the British House of Commons by a select committee on sugar and coffee planting, which was published in 1848. According to another source, Hopewell was in sugar cultivation in 1846. It then covered 1,865 acres and Palmetto Grove 1,040.[20] All these greater Woodside estates depended on the enslaved labour of Africans and Jamaicanized Africans.

By 1848, ten years after de facto emancipation, most of these estates had failed to be economically viable. The names that the owners gave their properties live on today, however, as we see from map 4, published in 1880 and revised in 1905, in 1917 and again in 1952. Notice that Palmetto Grove, Hopewell and the properties which came to represent the possessive terms Neilson's, Burrowes's, Turner's, Forbes's, and Harrison and Hart's, are positioned on the 1880 map as these names were on the map of 1804.

Chapter 2

The Business Career
of the Estates

Let us look at the business career of some of these places. We begin
with Woodside proper. By 1811 the spot marked Neilson's on the 1804
map had become known as Woodside, being listed in the official annual
returns as such. These returns were rather like today's income tax returns
but were made to the Vestry, that parish-based entity charged with a
degree of political and administrative responsibility. The reports were
published in the *Jamaica Almanack*. According to these returns,
Woodside was owned by W.J. Neilson. W.J. – William John – was the
son of Frances Maidstone and her husband John Neilson, who died in
1800 and whose tomb is in Woodside proper. On this estate in 1811
there were 153 slaves and 126 head of livestock.[1] W.J. Neilson, described
in his will[2] as a "practitioner of physic and surgery", extended his
estate in 1817 to the north of his gate with the purchase of land which
had belonged to Alexander Wright.[3] Upon review he must have con-
cluded that some of his property was now inconveniently located for in
1819 he made an agreement with James Dean to exchange twenty-four
acres of land close to Palmetto Grove for a piece of the same size close
to Hopewell. Neilson's Woodside property with this arrangement now
abuts Hopewell.[4]

There are changes in Neilson's business too: the number of slaves increased by nine to 162 in 1821, but the number of stock decreased by thirty-six.[5] By 1826 the number of slaves had increased once more by twenty-two to become 184, and the number of stock decreased again, this time by six, to eighty-four.[6] Neilson had obviously decided to move Woodside out of livestock. He could also have been trimming his land-holding too, for the 1826 increase in slaves is due in part to the transfer of eight slaves from his holding in St Thomas-in-the-Vale, the parish which adjoins St Mary.[7]

Neilson made other important decisions too, for on 17 December 1828, he signed his will, one clause of which decreed that his estate should go to his eldest son George and his wife Jane Eliza, and after, to his younger son William John, should George predecease him.[8] In that year, 1828, the number of slaves at Woodside proper went down by nine to 175, and stock went down once more, this time to fifty-eight.[9] But its business seemed to be thriving, for it was trading with London (England), Port Maria, Cape Clear Estate, Hopewell Pen and Richmond Estate, and sold an entire house worth £80 to Farquaharson in St Elizabeth.[10]

By June 1829 Dr William John Neilson was dead and the returns for his estate filed and signed by two of his executors, who recorded the transfer of fourteen slaves from his estate to his widow, Jane Eliza, on the grounds that they had been her private property.[11] A slave was sold too, in that year, to someone who might have been a family member, T. Neilson.[12] In 1830 the estate sold more of its livestock. Colts, mares, steers and fillies were sold to various persons, including Mr MacKay of Hampshire Estate, a surname we will meet later. By 1832 the number of slaves had gone down to 162.[13] Holdings in stock had gone down, now holdings in slaves were going down! The annual returns for 1832 show a John Ewart owning a small estate called Woodside in the neighbouring parish of St Thomas-in-the-Vale.[14] This is a new listing. Woodside's owner, it seems, had sold that part of the estate which is in St Thomas-in-the-Vale, and from which he had in 1826 transferred eight slaves. His St Thomas-in-the-Vale holding had been the area in today's St Catherine which we call Pear Tree Grove.

Woodside, now a property of 734 acres, was one of the estates in Jamaica officially listed between 1832 and 1848 as "abandoned coffee estate".[15] Nevertheless, Woodside still sold coffee after 1832, and it continued to sell out its remaining livestock. These sales amounted to £1,029

18s. 4d., according to the estate account filed in 1835.[16] The crop account for 1836–37 admits to having a stock of 14,093 pounds of coffee and to making sales of several items totalling £129 16s. 8d.[17]

Apart from coffee, Woodside made money from the sale of labour. In 1830[18] it had sold labour, amounting to £73 4s., for opening up lands at Orange River nearby; £113 1s. 3d. for labour sold to Non-such Estate; £24 7s. 6d. for day labour; and £142 17s. 6d. for labour on the highways, a total in excess of £350 for extra-estate work of its slaves. In 1836–37[19] it sold mason labour to Rock Spring and carpentry and mason labour to some other unspecified place. It also sold labour to "St Mary", presumably the local government. These sales brought in £59 16s. 8d., a much smaller figure for labour than in preceding years. The estate earned £70 more in that year: two women bought the un-expired part of their bond for £35 each. Ominous, for such manumissions and the total freedom to come meant the end of a renewable source of income.

The emancipation of slaves, announced in 1834 and finally effective in 1838, found Woodside's coffee and livestock business on the decline; loss of enslaved labour available for jobbing would have hurt it further, especially as this source had been self-perpetuating. The executrix, the widow of Dr Neilson, late of Woodside, signed the estate accounts herself in 1835. It would not be surprising if Mrs Jane Eliza Neilson's motive for being so actively engaged in running of the estate was to cut costs and/or review the estate's finances.

The Palmetto Grove plantation, a sugar producer, suffered similar and even more drastic change than Woodside, in that it changed hands. This holding of 1,040 acres was officially listed in the Vestry returns for 1811 as one entity belonging to Alexander Wright.[20] He had 243 slaves and 126 head of livestock. By 1817, unable to honour a mortgage, he had to alienate a portion of his land, which eventually went to the Neilsons.[21] In 1821 the property was listed as an estate separate from a pen.[22] It was now the property of James Dean, who had apparently decided to diversify. The estate was the larger part of the business, having 241 slaves and 111 stock, whereas the pen only had 20 slaves and no listed stock.

In 1826 the stock on the estate increased by thirty-three but the number of slaves decreases by seven, to 232.[23] The pen gained slaves: it now had twenty-seven. In 1828 the slave population on the pen remained unchanged but the figures for the estate increased:[24] there were 240 slaves on the estate and 153 head of livestock. By 1832 there was no longer a distinction between pen and estate, James Dean was now a "trustee", and there were 232 slaves and only 45 head of stock.[25] This estate was officially listed in this year as an abandoned sugar plantation and once again changed owners. By 1840 it was no longer associated with Dean; it was now the property of M.J. Purrier.[26]

When in 1784 there was a land dispute between the Parkers and the Grants, William Burrowes's land seems to have been a boundary of the land under question.[27] If this is so, then Burrowes clearly had been an owner in the area since 1784. It was no doubt he who brought those two Mary Gould mango trees and planted them in Rock Spring to form his gateway after, we presume, he had bought the larger part of his estate – one hundred acres – from the Parker family.[28] The map below outlining the boundaries of Burrowes's plantation calls it "Rock Spring" but since it is undated, it cannot tell us how old the name is.

It was not until 1821, in the annual returns reported in the *Jamaica Almanack,* that the name Rock Spring makes its dateable appearance. In that year it was the property of Mrs P.E. Burrowes, mother quite likely, wife perhaps, sister-in-law perhaps, of that "excellent young man" Edward Marchant Burrowes, who died in his thirty-first year. The estate continued to be in this woman's hands until 1840.[29] Rock Spring's business was small. In the years 1821 to 1832, according to its returns to the Vestry, it had between forty-four and fifty-four slaves and between none and two head of livestock.[30] Like Woodside, it had been a coffee-growing area, and between 1832 and 1848 this crop was abandoned. It also seems to have been broken up, because the lands acquired by Alexander Cooke, its 1840 owner, were but one hundred acres, and Rock Spring was, in 1832, a plot of 120 acres and in the undated map, 130 acres (see map 5).[31] The Burrowes name continued until 1839 to be mentioned in business transactions in the greater Woodside area.[32] Mary Burrowes was one of the recipients of five ten-acre plots disbursed by Richard Thomas of Smailfield in 1839.[33]

Smailfield, the property of the Turners, as we see from the map of 1804, was also a relatively small estate, though larger than Rock Spring.[34] Like Rock Spring it made no returns for the year 1811. It also made none for 1821. It did not do so until 1836, when it was listed in the Vestry returns as the property of John Crossman.[35] Crossman had,

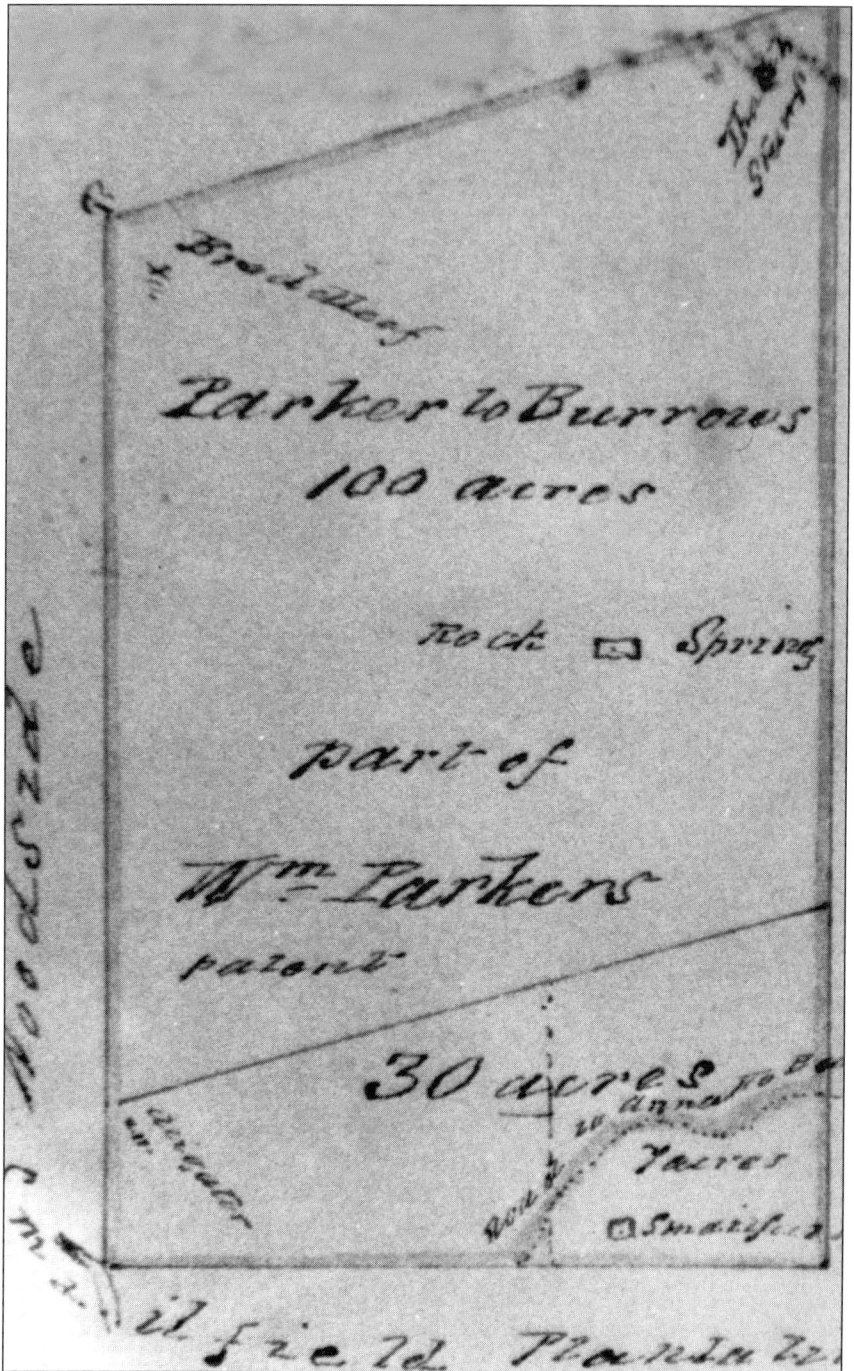

Map 5 Rock Spring (National Library of Jamaica)

Map 6 Smailfield Plantation (National Library of Jamaica)

from 1806 or before, bought the 148 acres of Orange River property that shared Smailfield's boundary. He put this with Smailfield's 180 acres to make a greater plantation of 328 acres. The original 180 acres had been the Turners' property until 1801, when tragedy struck the family. As can be seen from map 6, the area around the Great House was, from 1806, called Smailfield; so was the plantation.

In 1806 Smailfield was a well-ordered plantation, as we see from the diagram above, with five different plots in coffee amounting to fifty-six acres. It had ten acres of plantain, a pasture of more than thirty-two acres, Negro grounds and provision grounds in excess of fifty-five acres;

more than fifteen acres in woodlands and a great house on more than two acres. It makes no returns for 1811 and 1821. Did Crossman leave the property fallow until 1826? In that year Smailfield had seventy-one slaves and sixty head of stock. Business picked up: in 1828 Crossman got three more slaves and fourteen more head of cattle. But by 1832 Smailfield had passed out of the hands of John Crossman and was now the property of Maria Jane Pope; it now had just sixty-three slaves and fifty head of livestock.[36]

Smailfield became the property of Richard Thomas in about 1840.[37] It too is one of the estates that claimed to have abandoned coffee between 1832 and 1848.[38] It still had some coffee in 1839, though: its crop account admitted to forty-five hundred pounds of coffee "in hand".[39] This estate, which had recently lost its owner, Richard Thomas, through death, was selling out its heifers, cows, horned stock, a horse and a mule, and had made £408 for the year preceding. This account is signed by a James Smith before a John Douglas.

Louisiana was another coffee estate that was abandoned between 1832 and 1848.[40] This estate, listed as being in the parish of St Thomas-in-the-Vale until 1866, first appears by this name in the Vestry reports, the available records for the nineteenth century, in 1821. It was owned by James and Peter Burnett.[41] It stayed in the Burnett family until 1840 if not later.[42] In 1826 it was the property of Peter and Louisa Burnett,[43] giving substance to the oral report that the property was named for the wife of the proprietor.[44] In 1821 the Burnetts had 119 slaves and forty-five head of stock; in 1826 they had 131 slaves and thirty-six head of stock; in 1828 they had 125 slaves and twenty-six head of stock and in 1832, 133 slaves and 24 head of stock.[45]

Despite the hardships, Louisiana's affairs were not the sole responsibility of the family in 1832–33[46] and 1837: they could afford managerial help.[47] The earlier account was signed by Horatio Feurtado, the later by William Peterswold. In 1839 Sam Rogers was the overseer signing the crop accounts.[48] Coffee was the main item listed:[49] the estate now had "7 tierces and one cask containing coffee of 6023 [pounds]", more coffee than Smailfield had. Like Woodside, this estate made some money by trading with its neighbours, and selling labour. In 1832–33 Nancy Redwood was hired out to J.R. Forbes Esq., quite likely the John R. Forbes of Waterton, for £16; fifty pounds of coffee were sold to Petersfield plantation. In 1837 cattle as well as plantains, corn and cof-

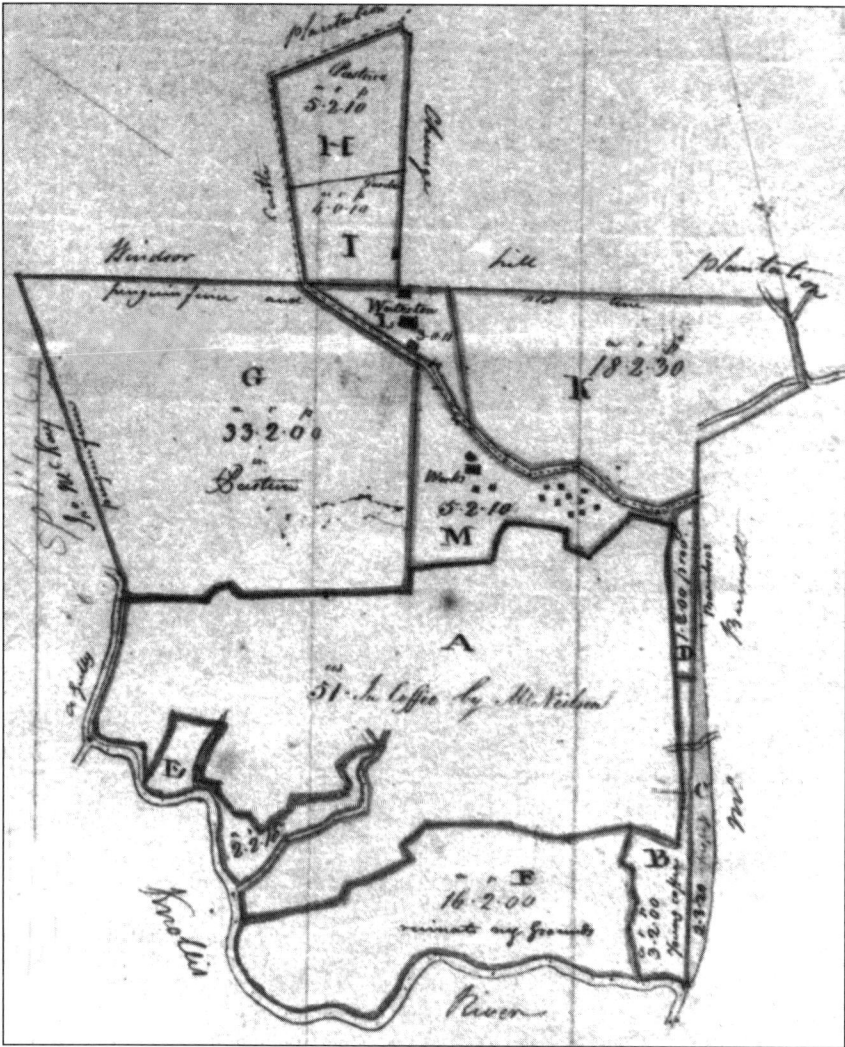

Map 7 Waterton Estate (National Library of Jamaica)

fee were sold, and coffee exchanged for sugar with Petersfield. The
Louisiana of today, reckoning from the position of Woodside, Rock
Spring and Smailfield, areas established by the presence of gravestones,
would be where, in 1804, we see the name Parker's.

Was this property not used until the Burnett's owned it or did it
operate under a different name? Interpreting the black blocks on the
map of 1804 to designate residences, we note that though the Burnetts

had had land in greater Woodside since 1777, they had no residence there.[50] We however note their presence in 1806, as seen on the map of Waterton; proof that they owned property but no clear proof one way or another that they lived there then. Waterton (map 7), where the Flint River begins, is represented on the map of 1804 by the name J. Forbes (map 3).

At this time it was just 148 acres and its largest section was devoted to coffee "by Mr Neilson". Only six other acres were in coffee; the rest were in provision grounds and pasture. A little more than five acres was assigned to works and Negro houses. The great house sat on three acres of land, probably atop the 102 steps leading today from Butler Spring to the area facing today's Change Hill. This estate does not appear in the records as making returns to the Vestry until 1821, when we see it as the property of two people – Elizabeth Forbes and John Forbes.[51] She owned twelve slaves; he owned sixteen, and twenty-one head of live-stock. We meet this estate again in the year 1826 when only the name, "John R Forbes", appears alongside Waterton.[52] Now he owns thirty-six slaves and fourteen head of cattle. It did its official duty again in 1828, once more in the names of Elizabeth and John R. Forbes.[53] This time she owns fifteen slaves and he twenty-six, and five head of cattle.

The 1840 listing of property owners as printed in the parish Vestry returns divided Waterton between Elizabeth and Isabella Forbes.[54] The estate was again in the records in 1848 but this time as one of the abandoned coffee estates.[55] At this time the estate was of 227 acres and had forty-four labourers. Waterton under the management of John Stevens[56] looked active in the crop report submitted in February of 1838. It had sold coffee to a William Morgan, to William Forbes Senior and to "Mrs Forbes" amounting to £255 16s. From jobbing its apprentices, about to be totally free in the coming year, it had made £57 8s. 6d. Still in hand were 4,638 pounds of coffee and a bushel of corn; the corn was worth £5 10s.

Waterton is between Louisiana and Windsor Castle on one of today's roads and between Windsor Castle and Change Hill on another. Though school records for 1928–48 do not mention this area as feeding Woodside School and though Mr Kelly's report does not mention it, it is hardly likely that children would have come to Woodside School from the two adjoining districts, further away in one case, and none come from Waterton. Since we are using the school's feeder area as the boundaries of the district of Woodside, on the assumption that Waterton is one of these areas, we have included it in greater Woodside. This estate, like Woodside, Rock Spring, Louisiana and Smailfield, went out of coffee growing on a commercial basis between 1832 and 1848. It spanned 228 acres.

Richmond Hill is one of the areas from which Woodside School got students in 1928–48. No such name appears in the records of returns made to the Vestry for 1811 and 1821, but we find it in 1824 listed in the returns to the Vestry as belonging to William Patterson, who owns thirty-nine slaves and twenty-two head of livestock and also owns Prospect Hill, where he has thirteen slaves.[57] It disappears from the returns again but we find news of it through its estate record for 1831, which tells us that it is shipping coffee to London and to Kingston.[58] This account is signed by Donald Patterson, likely to be a relative of William Patterson, its 1824 owner. We find it listed once more in the *Jamaica Almanack* among existing estates for the year 1840. It appears too in the list of the coffee-growing estates abandoned in or about 1832.[59] At that time it comprised 172 acres; its size remained the same in 1840. It is listed here as the property of John McPherson and as having seventy-seven labourers. The area we today call Richmond Hill, judging from its relationship to the places whose locations we identified by tombstones, would be between the Flint River and the Knollis River and would be part of "Parker's" of the 1804 map. Parker's we have already assumed to be Louisiana. Was Richmond Hill cut off from the Parker's property and sold after 1804 to the Pattersons?

Stapleton, another of those areas from which students came to Woodside School and which we include in the greater Woodside area, is even more absent from the records: it does not even appear in the list of 1840. It appears, however, in the list published in 1848, of estates abandoned "since 1832".[60] By the process of reconstruction that we have been using, today's Stapleton comprises the areas signalled on the 1804 map as the properties of Cunningham, Benwell and Pollock. A Pollock – Walter Pollock – in 1811 owned Flemington and Braemar, areas which are adjacent to today's Stapleton.[61] On Braemar he had 140 slaves and twenty-six head of livestock. On Flemington, he had just one slave. Several Pollocks make returns in 1821.[62] Three of them have only one or two slaves and nothing else. The "estate" of a Walter Pollock is mentioned as having two slaves and Flemington is listed as belonging to Walter Pollock, who here has only two slaves and no stock.

There is no mention at all at this time of Braemar, which by 1824 is now the property of Alexander McLauchlan, who owns forty-six slaves and eleven head of livestock.[63] There is no more news of Flemington and Braemar, and still no reference to Stapleton as an economic unit making official returns, until its mention as one of the non-functioning coffee estates of the early pre- and early post-emancipation period.[64] It is said then to be of 108 acres, with a labour pool of twenty. But we do know that it was an entity in 1829. Reference is made to it in another map of the area, in the discussion of the intended sale of Flemington Pen to Alexander Clarke.[65] This pen is described as bordered by Rose Hill and Flint River Pen, Brimmer, Stapleton and Alexander Clarke.

Though Windsor Castle had existed by this name since 1806, as we see from the map of Waterton above, its first mention in the returns to the Vestry after 1799 was for the year 1824.[66] It was owned then by John Crossman, who at that time also owned Smailfield, Hazard, Decoy and Decoy Pen. He had seventy-nine slaves at Windsor Castle and seventy-four head of livestock.[67] According to the returns for 1826, John Crossman still had his multiple estates, but now Decoy and Windsor Castle were grouped together and had 335 slaves and 194 head of livestock.

Mention of Windsor Castle in the returns ends here. Decoy Estate and Pen, and Hazard and Smailfield are still grouped together. They are now owned by Maria Jane Pope. Whatever happened to Windsor Castle? It seems to have been a livestock pen in 1824. Did it continue to be so, and why did Maria Jane Pope not get this estate as well as the others in John Crossman's group? What we do know is that by 1843, 232 acres of the Windsor Castle property have become a settlement of small owners, possibly ex-slaves.[68]

Petersfield and Brae Head were also areas in which children attending Woodside School between 1928 and 1948 lived. Judging from their present relationship to the areas whose identities in 1804 have been firmly established, these two areas would have been part of that section of greater Woodside that is marked on the 1804 map "Harrison and Hart's". Neither of these places submitted any returns for the years 1811–32, but we do know from other sources that Petersfield had its cadre of enslaved labour in this period, and that a Peter McCrae resided at Brae Head and did own seven slaves in 1817.[69] Three of his seven slaves who were baptized in the Anglican faith in 1817 carry his name, suggesting that he could have been their first Jamaican owner. One of the other four is a Neilson, possibly bought from neighbours. The other three, with surnames Bryan, Cannon and Christian, must have been bought further afield, for the greater Woodside area has no property owners with these surnames. Like Brae Head, Petersfield existed in 1817:[70] we see it used to define land being sold to Dr Neilson of Woodside.

Brae Head and Petersfield are listed in the 1840 compendium of properties and property owners.[71] From this we learn that in 1840 a Peter McCrae owns Brae Head, which is twenty acres in size. This would have to be Peter McCrae the second, for an earlier one died in 1829 and his estate was under the executorship of William Peterswold, a name we have met before.[72] The records also tell us that at this time Walter Pollock owned Petersfield, an estate of four hundred acres. We have met this surname, if not the person, before: it is associated with the ownership of Braemar, Flemington and the area that we assume to be today's Stapleton. Is this the same Walter Pollock who now owns Petersfield? And did he buy it from Peterswold? If yes, when did Peterswold buy it? We notice that in 1836 a William Peterswold, who a year later signs the Louisiana estate's accounts,[73] does an exchange in which Petersfield's sugar is swopped for Louisiana's coffee.[74] Was he an overseer on the Burnett's property while master of Petersfield?

A map of 1812[75] shows a William Peterswold as owning a part of what appears to be today's Petersfield and the former Harrison–Hart run, and leasing another run. A map of 1836[76] indicates that he has bought four hundred of these acres, which are bounded on the north-east by Woodside plantation, on the north-west by Carron Hall and Palmetto Grove, and on the south by Change Hill. In this same year, Peterswold is conveying Cottage, that piece of land "bordered by the Rio Sambre and by Petersfield and Palmetto Grove estate", thirty-one acres in size "formerly belonging to Petersfield plantation now differentiated into Cottage", to members of his family.[77] Was this four hundred acres all of the Harrison–Hart run? And is this the portion which becomes the property of Walter Pollock in 1840?

Whether a Peterswold was the owner of all the "Harrison and Hart's" land which we today call Petersfield or not, and if so when, is conjecture but there is no guessing about the involvement of a Peterswold in the greater Woodside area. It is a William Peterswold who, in 1817, sold to William John Neilson a piece of Palmetto Grove belonging to Wright and forfeited to him, along with its slaves. "Wold" in Old English is "field". It is very tempting to conclude that Petersfield bought some of the Harrison–Hart land from 1811, when we find the name in the government records, and named it Petersfield. And the greater Woodside patriarch need not even be the William named, since there is evidence that the Peterswolds have been in St Mary since 1809, at which time John William owned 241½ acres in the parish.[78] The reference does not say whether this St Mary land was the Harrison–Hart run.

The *Jamaica Almanack* gives Peter McCrae slaves but no landed property. It is only in 1829 that he appears in another source as the owner of Brae Head. It could be, then, that it was on his property that the Baptists who catered to the slaves had their religious meetings in February of 1831 and before.[79] The land, as we have already noted, was under the control of Peterswold as executor in 1829. Was he still in charge in 1831? Was it he who was sympathetic to the slaves and their need for religious expression, and accordingly gave their minister permission to use Brae Head? Was it Peter McCrae, deceased in 1829, who was the humane one or was it the Peter McCrae listed in 1840 as the owner of Brae Head who cooperated with the slaves and their religious leader?

Today's Change Hill is very close to today's Petersfield and Windsor Castle. The 1806 map of Waterton gives its location: it abutted that estate at two points on its northerly border. Given what we know of the 1804 position of Waterton and Woodside, Change Hill would be west of the area marked on that map "Harrison and Hart's". This is a large area; the only black block close by is marked "W. Neilson's". Was this large property Neilson's in 1804, when the survey was done? "W" no doubt refers to William Neilson, who was a surveyor practising in St Mary at the time. We have noted in chapter 1 that John Neilson owned what looks like part of this area in 1801. Was this land jointly owned by the Neilsons?

Whatever the story of its ownership, Change Hill was in production, for it was listed in the 1811 returns of the Vestry as published in the *Jamaica Almanack*. It was not, however, W. or any other Neilson who owned it then. In 1811 it was one of the group of properties owned by John Crossman.[80] The others were Windsor Castle, Hazard and Decoy

Pen. Here in Change Hill, Crossman owned 173 slaves and 136 head of cattle. In 1824 a Thaw was its owner. We find no other official reference to Change Hill there again until 1840 when it is listed among the existing properties in St Mary.[81] According to the 1840 reference, it was now owned by William Tucker. Change Hill, however, must have remained a viable economic unit at least until 1818, for it did register the baptisms of fifty-five enslaved persons in 1817 and 1818.[82]

Hopewell, like Palmetto Grove, gives us no difficulty to locate. They exist as place names on the earliest detailed map of St Mary that we have been able to find, the 1804 map. Hopewell belonged to the Honourable Charles Grant, whom, we have already noted, was custos of St Mary in 1804 and one of the two members of the legislature for the parish of St Mary. That the space had a name indicates that it was developed before 1804. In fact, Lady Nugent and her husband, then governor of Jamaica, visited it in 1802 and described its house as "a very good one, everything neat about it, and it commands a view of a very beautiful country".[83] The estate, according to her, was "worth clear £18,000 per annum".[84]

Hopewell Estate and/or Hopewell Pen appears in the list of returns for every period covered by this chapter and has been consistently the property of Charles Grant or his heirs.[85] In 1811 it reported having 414 slaves and 457 head of stock; clearly a pen. The 1821 returns separate it into estate and pen, the estate having 310 slaves and 286 head of livestock and the pen having 106 slaves and 146 head of livestock. In 1824 the estate had 305 slaves and 289 head of livestock and the pen 106 slaves and 144 head of livestock. Charles Grant must have died shortly after, for in 1832 the returns now appear in the name of "heirs of Chas. Grant". There are still very many slaves on the estate but no livestock listed. There are now 90 slaves on the pen and 147 head of livestock. Hopewell Pen in 1840, and most likely before that, stretched over five hundred acres of land, and the sugar estate over thirteen hundred acres. On the 1804 map there are three contiguous properties listed as "C. Grant's". These are separated from Hopewell by Orange River and from Turner's by White Gut. Is this C. Grant the owner of Hopewell?

The data above indicate that apart from Hopewell Estate and Pen, which were about seventeen hundred acres, and Palmetto Grove, which was 1,040 acres, the Woodside estate or Woodside proper was the largest of the holdings in greater Woodside between 1811 and 1840, and certainly the largest of the surrounding coffee estates. Its early-twentieth-century pre-eminence, judged by the fact that the primary school and the Anglican church were sited there, was therefore long-standing. The rest of this work will focus on Woodside proper, though references will be made from time to time to greater Woodside.

Chapter 3

The White People of Greater Woodside, 1799–1838

The Men

Jamaica, like the rest of the so-called New World since the seventeenth century, had used transported and enslaved labourers from Africa for personal and business purposes. This system of slave labour came to an official end in 1838 with the Emancipation Proclamation of 1 August of that year, the final stage in a process that began with the Abolition Act of 1 August 1834. The use of this kind of labour to develop the island meant that between 1755, where our review of the relevant records begins, and emancipation, there were, broadly speaking, two kinds of people in Jamaica and in Woodside — the free and the slave. The system was upheld by the law: all white people were free and nearly all blacks were enslaved, so that for references to "slave", we can without contradiction read "enslaved person of African descent, usually black-skinned but sometimes brown and even near white". Very few blacks/browns owned lands; fewer held any official position in the period 1755–1840. On some of the documents consulted for this period signatories specifically declared themselves to be "coloured". None of the persons discussed below have made any such confession. The probability is high that this discussion of posts held by Woodside people relates only to its white residents. Information concerning these posts for the period 1755–1840 comes to us from the *Jamaica Almanack.*

John Neilson, the owner of Woodside and who died in 1800, held an important post. In 1799 he was a major in the St Mary regiment and had been so since 29 May 1796. Such a position would have made Neilson a respected person in the area. Absenteeism was not the style of coffee planters, so at whatever other job he worked, we expect that John Neilson was around in Woodside running his estate and riding in his major's uniform to meet with other officers for military exercises within the parish. The register of deeds at the Government Records Office in Spanish Town show that there were two Neilsons involved in property transfers in Jamaica in the eighteenth century. There was George Neilson, who in 1775 had business transactions with William Reynolds,[1] and John Neilson who did business in 1785 with Robert Kincaid.[2] Neither of these transactions had anything to do with Woodside or with St Mary. Did Woodside's John Neilson have property outside of St Mary? Did brothers with the same surname migrate to Jamaica, some settling in the greater Woodside area? A George Neilson registered his will[3] in 1755, but this was in too bad a condition at the time of this research to be read. Was George John Neilson's father?

There is also a William Neilson listed in the *Jamaica Almanack* of 1796 as a surveyor. This is no doubt the W. Neilson who, according to the map of 1804, then lived near to North Palmetto Grove, and whom we mentioned in the preceding chapter. It is quite likely this William Neilson to whom Frances Neilson – widowed by John's death in 1800 at age sixty-one years – entrusts the property passed down to his son William John in 1801.[4] William John was about ten years old at the time. William the elder was asked to oversee his property for eleven years until William John attained majority; his mother went to England and he, we assume, went with her.

The assumption that there was a kinship relationship between John and William is very tempting in view of the fact that John's son is William John. Were John and William sons of George? William John subsequently named his heir "George". Did he name him for his grandfather, who was in business in Jamaica in 1775? If yes, then the Woodside Neilsons had been in Jamaica for two decades before Frances Neilson sold her slave to her neighbour William Parker in 1798.[5]

While John Neilson was serving in the regiment as a major, a William

Burrowes served as assistant judge. This would have been a position reserved for the wisest and therefore the oldest, the assumption of a positive relationship between age and wisdom being even more popular then than it is today. This William Burrowes had property in the greater Woodside area earlier than 1785 and as we see from the black block on the 1804 map, lived here. He is likely to have been the father of the thirty-one-year-old Edward Marchant Burrowes who died in 1812 and was mourned by his sister. William Burrowes exited the records in 1799 and had probably died, leaving his son Edward and his widow and daughter to manage Rock Spring.

There was another William Burrowes around in 1804, associated with Stony Hill in St Andrew, a neighbouring parish. He was assistant staff surgeon in the regiment and his wife was close enough to the governor's wife to have had tea with her and to be mourned on her passing by this great personage.[6] How were these Burrowes related to the Edward Marchant of Rock Spring, born in 1781? Another Burrowes, Edward M. Burrowes, appeared in the property returns for 1821 as owner of Villa Estate, plus thirty slaves and four head of livestock. This place was in St Thomas-in-the-Vale, the parish which adjoined St Mary up until 1866 when it ceased to exist, being absorbed into the parish of St Catherine. How was this one related to Edward Marchant, who died in 1812? Was this a cousin or an uncle from whom he got his initials, or was this a son of his early years, to whom he gave his initials?

Another Burrowes appears in the records as well. He is M. Burrowes. He, like William Burrowes, is a military man: he is quartermaster for the Eastern St Mary troops in 1808. Is he brother to the William of Rock Spring? It was popular then to give children the first names of the father or mother's brother or sister as their first or middle name. Could the M. Burrowes above be a Marchant Burrowes, brother to Rock Spring's William, brother to Edward M. and uncle to Edward Marchant? There is yet another Burrowes. This is Miss S.J. Burrowes, who owns no landed property but, according to the returns for 1821, owns eight slaves. This kind and quantum of property remains until 1832. Edward M. is the agent of both Miss P.E. and Miss S.J. Burrowes. He signs the slave returns of 1820 as such.

Whatever the kinship lines, what is clear is that William Burrowes, among other Burroweses, was, like John Neilson, part of the armed forces which protected St Mary, and greater Woodside in particular.

Probably, like and with Neilson, he travelled from and through Rock Spring to the barracks, which on the map of 1804 is close to Hopewell. In their absence from home, wife and/or overseer would have seen to their coffee estates.

There were more Neilsons than there were Burrowes in the official lists for greater Woodside in the period before emancipation. There was William John, who was a captain in the St Mary regiment in 1817 and certainly until 1828. There was also a James H. Neilson, who was a deputy judge advocate in 1822 and who was, by 1828, an assistant judge. This James H. was also a member of the Vestry. At the time he owned no landed property, only six slaves. Was he the son of William the elder, who owned lands and a residence in the area that seems to be Change Hill, and who was charged with taking care of William John's inheritances until he came of age? This William, a surveyor, we suspect to be the brother of William John's father. If our suppositions are right, then James H. would be the cousin of William John. Whatever their kin relationship, they were socially close, for Dr Neilson is one of the bridal party at James's wedding on 24 June 1821 to a lady whose name is given only as Maria Louisa.[7] This lady, a spinster, is from St Mary. The marriage took place at Carron Hall, an area now adjacent to Change Hill.

By 5 August the James H. Neilsons were again in the company of Dr Neilson, and not only he but his wife and his mother, "Mrs Neilson Sr", whom we recognize as Frances Maidstone. This time they were at the wedding of Hugh Donald MacKay, who signed himself in 1830 as the overseer on the Woodside estate.[8] By 1835 Dr William John had died, leaving a wife and six children, none of whom was over twenty-one years of age.[9] Woodside and St Mary lost, with his death, a doctor of physic and surgery, one who had been captain in the militia from 1817 to 1828, and assistant judge from 1811, when he attained his majority, to 1828.[10]

Apart from the Woodside, the Change Hill and possibly the Carron Hall Neilsons there were also Neilsons in an area close to greater Woodside, Dunkeld. This area was in the adjoining parish of St Thomas-in-the-Vale. How was Margaret B., with property at Dunkeld, related to the Woodside Neilsons? In 1826 she had eighteen slaves. James H. also owned slaves in this parish as well as in St Mary. There was also in Dunkeld another William Neilson, who owned slaves but no landed property.

There was a Turner as a landowner from as early as 1785. He might have recently bought and not yet given the name "Smailfield" to his property, for it is by his name that his property is referred to as one of the boundaries to land then being surveyed.[11] This looks very much like the William Turner who died in 1801. In 1799, when John Neilson was a major in the regiment and William Neilson and J. Neilson, possibly his nephews, were ensigns, William Turner, Neilson's neighbour at Smailfield, was a captain in the regiment. He was at the time forty-three years old, a youngster to John Neilson, who was then sixty years old. Two years later a tragedy hit the family: Turner died on the same day as his son, who was then aged five. He did not get to see the reference to his name in the *Jamaica Almanack*; there is a cross beside it.

After 1801 the Turner name appeared neither in the property returns made to the Vestry of the parish nor in the lists of officers of the Vestry, the judiciary or the military. We note, however, that on 13 September 1821 it made its appearance in association with that of the Neilsons.[12] On that day, at Woodside, Isabella Turner gave her hand in marriage to Charles Seymour Cockburn of St Andrew. In the wedding party were Dr and Mrs Neilson. There was no mention of a father Turner, mother Turner, or any other Turner at the wedding. Did the widow of William Turner leave Smailfield by decease or migration after erecting the monument to her husband, and leave behind a daughter in the care of the Neilsons? The other members of the wedding were John Crossman Esq. and Mrs Crossman. This is the John Crossman in whose hands we find Smailfield, along with a number of other estates in and around greater Woodside, in 1824. Mrs Turner must have left her affairs in the hands of Dr Neilson, her neighbour, and John Crossman, who was possibly a real estate attorney and who certainly served as early as 1811, with Neilson, as a member of the parish judiciary.

The owners of these contiguous coffee estates and their families – the Neilsons, the Burrowes and the Turners – were to one extent or another associated with the regiment. In Jane Austen's England, a system of transmission of property by which estates were passed intact to the eldest son forced younger sons into the professions to make a living, and to establish their own land-based holdings and their own dynasties. One profession available to them was the army. The availability of land in the colonies encouraged this practice. It is possible that John Neilson, William Turner and the first Burrowes were career army officers who chose service in Jamaica in the hope of establishing themselves here as planters.

The first phase of British development of Jamaica is also associated with the military. That first plan for the settlement of the 2,823,174 acres of land called Jamaica, offered grants of thirty acres to any Britisher over twelve years of age who would guarantee to cultivate it. The earliest takers were soldiers in the army that had, in 1655, seized the island from Spain. Could these families whom we meet in the mid-eighteenth century have been the inheritors of a conceptual relationship between the agricultural development of a colonial possession and its protection by military action?

Whatever the reasoning behind their migration to Jamaica, and to the greater Woodside area, the fact is that there was a connection between the landowning families in the Woodside area and the regiment. We note a modern opinion concerning this period, that "coffee cultivation offered a means of increasing the number of small settlers in Jamaica and the other West Indian colonies as well, to strengthen the local militias against the threat of foreign invasions and slave revolts".[13]

We also note from this source that incentives were given to coffee planters in 1784 in the form of reduction of the excise duty. Clearly the conceptual connection between agriculture and the militia was still alive and well in the 1780s. The military had a reputation, then as now, as a good teacher of the discipline needed by healthy young men. On these grounds alone it would have been attractive to upwardly mobile British families cut off from British society and culture. Note too that the late eighteenth century was a period of international warfare in the Caribbean. Woodside's settlers would have been careless if they had not armed themselves, whether officially encouraged or not, as subsidiaries to a state army or as the major armed force. Let us see, however, whether the association of the landed in Woodside and greater Woodside with the regiment existed for other families.

Jonathan Forbes first appeared in the records in 1804. At this time Charles Grant of Hopewell was custos as well as assemblyman for the parish of St Mary. Other Grants were public servants as well. There were Peter and Alex, who sat with Charles in the Vestry. Jonathan Forbes sat with them as collecting constable. This Jonathan could also be the J. Forbes who, according to the 1804 maps, owned lands at the head of the Flint River, and the J. Forbes who, in 1804, was a major in the St

Mary regiment and who in 1806 ordered a drawing of his property, then called Waterton. There was also another W. Forbes who was associated with the military. He was in the artillery in 1799 and lieutenant colonel in the army in 1810. Is this the W. Forbes who was dead by 1811, and his property assessed? By this assessment his heirs owned Caledonia Estate in St Mary and forty slaves.

It is hardly likely that in such a small area as greater Woodside there would be at this time common surnames which do not indicate a kinship relationship. The question is, therefore: How are these several Forbes's related? Is Jonathan the son and heir of W. Forbes, or is he his brother? There is no more official word of a Jonathan until after emancipation, but in the returns for 1821 we see Elizabeth and John Forbes appearing as owners of Waterton, a place which is the same today as that spot on the 1804 map marked "J Forbes's". John and Elizabeth, whether they be siblings or mates, seem to be the heirs of Jonathan Forbes. If mates, it is more than likely that they produced a Jonathan, named after his grandfather, for we see this name on a late-nineteenth-century map of greater Woodside.

The 1804 map for St Mary also introduces us to another Forbes. He owns Donnington Castle, and is the health officer at Port Maria until 1814, if not later. This is clearly not the W. Forbes who died in 1811. There is also another W. Forbes, this one a churchwarden in 1814; again, not the W. Forbes who died in 1811. Who is related to whom we cannot tell from the sources available; what is clear, though, is that there were a number of early St Mary Forbes – two W. Forbes and a J. Forbes, quite likely Jonathan Forbes. Jonathan had property at Waterton and one of the others at Caledonia.

All three were contemporaries of John Neilson; W. Forbes was, like him, an officer in the regiment in St Mary. Their sons shunned the military, opting for more peaceful service, for by 1828 J.R. Forbes had become what William Forbes was in 1814, a churchwarden. J.R. – John R. – with Elizabeth continued the Forbes involvement with Waterton, a part of greater Woodside, until 1840, when John's name no longer appeared and Waterton was now in the charge of Elizabeth and Isabella. Were they aunt and niece, mother and daughter, or sisters? Isabella also owned at this time a seven-acre plot in St Thomas-in-the-Vale. The Forbes name continued to be associated with Waterton until well after emancipation in 1838.

John Crossman emerged in 1824 as the person in charge of five estates in St Mary, from two of which places children in the mid-twentieth century came to Woodside School: Windsor Castle and Smailfield. The other estates were Decoy, Decoy Pen and Hazard. By 1832 all these properties except Windsor Castle, for which no returns were submitted to the Vestry for that year, were the property of Jane Pope, and the Crossman name failed to show again until after emancipation in 1838. John Crossman Esq. had been, in 1811, along with William John Neilson, an assistant judge. He continued to be so in 1828, in which year he owned Change Hill and still owned Decoy Pen, Windsor Castle and Hazard. Being a member of the judiciary was Crossman's only reported association with public life. He held this position for many years beginning in 1811. It must have taken Crossman many years to acquire the five properties he owned in 1828. Did he own these properties, or did he manage them for clients who were indebted to him?

The Grant name, and in particular Charles Grant's, had been well-known in the greater Woodside area before 1799. By 1784 he was in dispute with John William Parker over land. This land was part of a four-thousand-acre run that the Crown had made available to John Bathurst for development on 9 June 1674, and whose patent Grant had taken over. By 1799 Grant was very well settled, certainly as far as status was concerned, for he was lieutenant colonel of the regiment and, as we know, was custos and assemblyman for the parish by 1804. These three roles meant frequent association with the governor and frequent visits to Spanish Town and its gay life. It also meant visits from the governor. His Hopewell home was graced at least once, in 1802, by Governor Nugent and his party.

There are several other Grants in the records. There is Peter Grant, an assistant judge in 1804, while Charles Grant is custos and assemblyman; there is an Alex Grant who by 1811 is also an assistant judge. These two are magistrates in 1814. A James Grant appears in 1808 as acting adjutant in the regiment. In 1822 David McD Grant and James Grant join a Charles Grant as assistant judges serving along with William John Neilson. With J.H. Neilson, David McD Grant is a vestryman, and a James Grant also works with Neilson, this time in the regiment where Grant is a captain and Neilson an ensign, and where William John Neilson is a lieutenant. Oddly enough, no other Grant except Charles makes returns for property in St Mary.

Were all these the children of a long-lived Charles Grant who passed away between 1826 and 1832, and whose considerable property was listed in 1832 as belonging to "heirs of Chas Grant"? On what salaries did these Grants survive? Was it from the government, with allowances from a father? They certainly were from a family that was closely related to the regiment, and the barracks where the regiment presumably met, was, according to the map of 1804, relatively close to Charles Grant's property.

W. Pollock Esq. was the coroner for St Mary in 1799. In 1804 a Walter Pollock was colonel in the regiment, sitting to dinner at the governor's house in Spanish Town. In 1811, while Charles Grant was lieutenant colonel in the St Mary regiment and John Neilson a major, a Walter Pollock was an assistant judge and a Walter Pollock was coroner and collecting constable. Were the two Walter Pollocks the same person? A Walter Pollock was the owner of Flemington and Braemar in 1802 and in 1811.[14] His name appears on the 1804 map in the spot that we today know as Flemington and Braemar. A Walter Pollock evidently owned these properties at the same time as Neilson, Burrowes, Turner, and J. Forbes had theirs.

By 1821 other Pollocks appear in the list of property owners besides Walter, but none seem to have followed his career in the military. The new Pollock property owners are Elizabeth and James, who have one slave each, and Jane, who has two. The estate of Walter Pollock has two slaves, and Flemington, the property of Walter Pollock, also has two. It seems that a Walter Pollock has passed on and left Flemington to a Walter Pollock, probably his son; Braemar has not been passed on. Perhaps the two slaves mentioned as belonging to the estate of Walter Pollock are left over from this latter property. In 1824 Braemar appears in the list of property returns as the possession of Alexander McLauchlan. The name Walter Pollock appears again elsewhere after emancipation in the list of property owners.

We meet Peter Burnett in 1814. He is a St Mary vestryman. James, perhaps his brother, is the collecting constable for the parish at that time. There is also a William who holds office, also in 1814; he too is a vestryman. It is Peter from this family that is of the regiment; there he is in 1809, a captain. There is no evidence that the Burnetts' property is producing until in 1821, when Peter and James are listed among the returns as owners of Louisiana Estate, then confined to St Thomas-in-the-Vale.

In 1824 James's name disappears from the list and Peter's is now twinned with "L.A." as owner of Louisiana. It becomes clear from the returns for 1826 that L.A. is Louisa, who is quite likely his wife after whom the estate is named. If this is so, as the oral reports claim, then Louisa would have been married to Peter from before 1821 when the first reference to Louisiana appears. By 1840 this estate comprises 384 acres, 181 of which are in the parish of St Mary, just above the Woodside estate.

Did the Burnetts of Louisiana buy these 181 acres from their closest neighbours in St Mary, the Neilsons? Oral sources claim that after the death of Dr William John, his widow and his heir sold out large acreages of the property. Unfortunately, though we know the size of Woodside in 1832, and in 1880 when the estate has lost only fifty-four acres, we do not know its size in 1829, the year of William John's death. We do know, though, that large parts of today's Woodside that abut Louisiana are officially registered as "part of Louisiana estate". Clearly Louisiana did extend itself into Woodside, but when did this happen? The rest of the Burnetts' 1840 possession is in St Thomas-in-the-Vale. Of all the residents in and about Woodside and greater Woodside, mentioned above, the Burnetts are the only ones who have left a place name to remind us of their existence. Today there is a place beyond Woodside and near to Louisiana that is called Burnett-land.

Neither James Dean nor any other Dean was a long-standing presence in the Woodside area, though James Dean was undoubtedly involved in business here and left his name to a district close to today's Palmetto Grove. There is evidence that James Dean was in a business deal with Dr William J. Neilson in 1819.[15] In this year there was an agreement between Dean and Neilson to exchange twenty-four acres of land from one property to the other. In spite of his status as owner of a property of more than one thousand acres, Dean was not an officer in the regiment, nor did he hold office in the Vestry; nor did any other person with his surname, while he owned Palmetto Grove, serve in the judiciary, the Vestry or the regiment. James Dean took over Palmetto Grove from Alexander Wright and kept the estate and pen, in its later stage, as "trustee", until 1840, when the sugar estate collapsed and the property was passed over to W.J. Purrier.

The Patterson name was also a relatively new one in greater Woodside. It began to be heard in 1824 when the Richmond Hill estate fell into Patterson hands. It maintained a presence until after emancipation. The Pattersons, with the Deans and Crossmans, are the only families that lived or owned property in Woodside or greater Woodside who were not at some time officers in the regiments for St Mary or for St Thomas-in-the-Vale. There is no evidence that they were here in the earliest decades of the nineteenth century. Their names do not appear on the map of 1804. Patterson and Dean make their appearance in the records we have consulted, only in the 1820s; Crossman is earlier –1806 in fact, when he seemed to be interested in acquiring Smailfield. After that he appeared as an owner of several properties and was at Woodside great house on 13 September 1821 for Isabella Turner's wedding to Charles Seymour Cockburn of Kingston, according to the register of births, deaths and marriages of the non-slave population in St Mary. Why was a family name so well-placed socially, not part of the officer corps of the militia, or even part of the militia? He might have been coloured or Jewish, groups which faced discrimination at that time. If he were coloured, it is quite likely that he would have stated this, as other slave owners did in the slave registers; but he did not. All the families that appear on the 1804 map were related to the regiment.

The historian Edward (Kamau) Brathwaite tells us that in 1681 an act was passed by which a militia was set up in the island.[16] Its purpose was to defend Jamaica from external aggressors and from slave rebellions. The militia was to consist of all local freemen, which meant that whites, blacks and Jews could be in it. Militia duty was compulsory. The officers of this militia were white, the expenses and influence involved being out of the reach of any others. Officers were commissioned by the governor. The commissions cost: to be a general cost £30; a colonel, £21; a major, £12 10s.; and to be an ensign, adjutant or quartermaster cost £3 5s. The Woodside area was clearly full of white people who could afford to buy commissions to become officers.

But it was not only money that allowed one to secure a commission: you had to be recommended by colonels of the militia. Woodside's white people, so many of whom were officers in the regiment, obviously belonged to that network of people known by the higher ranks of the militia, and themselves were bound together by membership in the public sector; they were judges, churchwardens and vestrymen. These men as members of the militia were not paid; they had to finance their own uniforms and arms. They are likely to have bought these from the same source – another occasion for bonding. In addition to expenditure on

arms and uniforms, these greater Woodside men had to give time for
monthly drills and quarterly field inspection. And it must have been a
sight for people in the Woodside area to see these powerful landowners
dressed in their military garb, complete with arms, riding on their expen-
sive horses – costing £50 each, according to Brathwaite quoted above –
making their way to the parade sites for inspection. This apart from anything else would constitute a show of force. These meetings would have
left no one in doubt about who was in charge in this area!

The white landowners – the Neilsons, the Forbes, the Pollocks and
to a lesser extent the Burrowes, and in an earlier period the Turners and
a later period the Burnetts – with posts in the Vestry, the judiciary and
the regiment, were the upper class of greater Woodside. There were lesser
whites too, people like the parents of Edmund Forbes of Rock Spring,
who was baptized in 1820. No Forbes appear as property owners in
Rock Spring over this period of time. How did they make their living
and what was their place in the social structure of the area? Similar questions can be asked of the parents of the Margaret Welch, Frank Leslie,
Mary Ann Hudson, and Mary and Ellen Fraser, all of whom were baptized in Hopewell in 1820, according to the records of births in the
Government Archives. These questions can also be asked concerning the
parents of Cecelia Grant and Joseph Anderson of Palmetto Grove, baptized in 1821. The baptismal records for this period tell us that these
people were neither "coloured" nor "slave": they were white. Their
names do not appear in the list of landowners making returns to the
Vestry. What were their jobs? They were probably tradesmen servicing
the coffee planters.

Other people likely to have been white and living and working in the
greater Woodside area between 1799 and 1838 were: Patrick Morgan,
who signed the Woodside Estate accounts in 1828, Hugh MacKay who
was its overseer in 1830, Horatio Feurtado, who signed the Louisiana
Estate accounts in 1837, William Peterswold, who signed them in 1837
and Sam Rogers, its overseer in 1838. Peterswold married Jane Gray at
Carron Hall the day before James Henry Neilson married his Maria
Louisa, also at Carron Hall.[17] Why were the Neilsons not listed as being
at Peterswold's wedding too? Hardly because he was of a lesser profession, because they were prominent at Hugh D. MacKay's wedding and
he was not a landed proprietor. History will have to keep this as a secret.

To this list of professionals we can add Alexander D. Cooke, who was a government physician in 1838 and lived at Rock Spring with his wife, Augusta, and his two daughters, Isabel and Ann Augusta, both of whom were baptized in 1838.[18] Alex D. Cooke MD was by then the owner of the Rock Spring property. We can also add Reverend J.W. Archer, island curate, who also lived at Rock Spring and who, prior to his death in 1841, crossed swords with the stipendiary magistrate Fyfe, who was also manager of a sugar estate near to Annotto Bay, on the issue of creating the parish of Metcalfe out of part of St Mary.[19] Obviously, to this list we must add Alexander Gordon Fyfe, who came to the area after 1835 and seemed to have also lived at Rock Spring, which is emerging as the residential section of the greater Woodside area.[20] A.G. Fyfe was very active in public life in St Mary and Jamaica in the post-emancipation era.[21] Add to this list the two clerks of J.H. and W.J. Neilson, Hugh Mason and Joseph Gray, the latter two buried as whites in 1821.

The Women

Frances Maidstone Neilson conceived William John Neilson by her husband John Neilson when he was fifty-one years old. At his death in 1800, ten years later, their heir was only nine years old. Given the age of her son and the fact of menopause, Frances Maidstone was probably much younger than her husband. His death left her with an estate to manage and a very young son to guide into the management of the Woodside property. Frances Maidstone Neilson, and possibly the Neilson family, must have had financially strong connections with Britain for that is where she went, probably with her son, after arranging in 1801, with one who appears to be his father's brother, to take over management of the estate for eleven years. Frances Maidstone had property in her own right. We find her selling a slave in 1798[22] and again in 1809.[23] Her son trained as a medical doctor and Mrs Neilson probably returned to Jamaica with him; she had slaves: eight in 1821, twelve in 1826 and fifteen by 1832. Mrs Neilson obviously returned to reside in Jamaica, for she signs slave returns in 1817, 1820, 1826, 1829 and even in 1832, and she had been at the wedding of Hugh Donald MacKay at Woodside in 1821. A care-taking relationship continued with her son, this time mother being the beneficiary: by his will of 17 December 1828[24] she was to get, for the rest of her life, an annual payment of £500.

Frances Maidstone's daughter-in-law was also now a widow. William John died at about forty years of age, leaving her with a very young family – four girls followed by two boys, all of them under twenty-one years of age. In 1828, when William John made his will, Jane Eliza was pregnant with a seventh child. This one must have died young, for there was no mention of this child in the 1833 document by which the inheritance of Helen Ismail, her eldest child, was passed over to her betrothed on her engagement. Helen Ismail, still a minor in 1833, was engaged to marry James Marshall.[25] According to her father's will, each child was due, at majority, £2,000. The estate, as we have noted in the preceding section, was going down. Jane Eliza made legal representation for Helen Ismail's money to be released to her intended husband. Do we see here a poverty-inspired panic, forcing Jane Eliza to release Helen's money before her majority in order to make her more eligible for marriage?

On the death of William John's mother, Frances, her £500 annuity was to be increased to £800 and put towards the support of the education of his children. From the number of Xs one sees in the records for that time beside women's names, literacy in women was unusual. Did Helen Ismail get a chance to make use of the provision in her father's will relating to the support of the education of his children? Jane Eliza was to get £1,000. The estate went jointly to her and his eldest son George, and, in the case of his death, was to pass to the younger son, William John. Both sons were pitiably young and unable to assume managerial responsibilities. Jane Eliza leaned heavily on Hugh Donald MacKay, a friend of the family who celebrated his marriage in 1821 at Jane Eliza's house.[26] It was with him that she made the arrangement for the release of Helen Ismail's money to her betrothed. It was he who signed Woodside's estate accounts in 1830, and does so again in the two years preceding full emancipation.[27]

Other men who might have come to the support of the widow and her many young children were neighbours who witnessed her husband's will – Peter Burnett of Louisiana, William T. Walker of the Carron Hall Walkers, and Mordecai Hart of the Harrison–Hart property close by. For his executor, William John had looked further afield. He chose George William MacKay of Springfield in the neighbouring parish, and William Andrews and Barnaby Maddan, both of Kingston, to assist Jane Eliza. William John was a medical doctor, so might have diagnosed a terminal illness in himself. A concern at this time would have been to find the best and most honest friends to serve as executors of his will. Less than a year after he had registered his will, and months after William John's death, William Andrews officially and in forthright language discharged himself from among the list of executors.[28] There was obviously a breach in the network of support around the widow.

Barnaby Maddan and MacKay, his fellow executor, sign the slave returns for the estate of Dr William John Neilson in 1829, and as mentioned before transfer a number of slaves from the deceased's estate to the widow on the grounds that they were her property. Like Jane Eliza Neilson, Maria Louisa Neilson lost her husband, whom she had wed in 1821 at Carron Hall in the presence of Jane Eliza and her husband. James H. Neilson had property in St Mary and in St Thomas-in-the-Vale. His wife, like Jane Eliza, also took over slaves from her deceased husband's estate in 1829, but these transfers were by sale.[29] Were Maddan and MacKay giving to Mrs Eliza Neilson what she should have bought, and was this what caused a breach in her support network? The loss of an executor was, however, a minor disturbance compared to the other problems that faced this widow, with three more daughters for whom to find worthwhile husbands and two sons to make into estate managers and/or professionals like their father.

William John had not been only the owner of the largest coffee plantation in greater Woodside, he had been a medical doctor who, it is logical to assume, had a practice that earned him money. That two of his original executors are from Kingston suggests that he had business in that part of the world, more than forty carriage miles away from Woodside. With his death, his love and care, his management skills and the additional source of income went. This at a time when there was talk of a social and economic revolution that would surely come with the emancipation of the slaves. This, a time of fear even of religious activity among slaves, when Sam Sharpe's rebellion of 1831 was casting its shadow and encouraging the Anglican clergy to contemplate preserving the status quo by banding themselves into the Colonial Church Union and burning nonconformist churches. The Baptist church in Port Maria, the mother church to that in greater Woodside, would actually be torched in 1835.[30] A little tinkering with her husband's will would not be enough: Jane Eliza's internal and external worlds were being shattered.

She stayed on in Woodside in these disturbing times, until 1842, if not later, to become a much-talked-about figure, presented in the oral reports even today as a proud woman for whose wedding a red carpet was spread from Woodside's gate to the house about two chains away; who would not take money from blacks except with a gloved hand, and who was brought so low that she would walk around the village with a calabash, begging salt from her former slaves, fed on roasted bananas by a man with a big leg ulcer, while her son and heir drank the family fortune away and left her to feed on lizards. With the personal and social revolutions facing Jane Eliza it would not be surprising if, as these reports suggest, she did indeed collapse mentally.

William Turner of Smailfield also predeceased his wife. Turner, who settled into Smailfield before he was twenty-nine years old, died in 1801 leaving a small but very well-organized estate. In 1806, fifty-five of its 180 acres were in woodlands and in provision grounds for its enslaved workers.[31] This was the area enclosed by the Flint River and the road to Spanish Town. At its northern end, near to Rock Spring, it had coffee and its works. There was also coffee across the road and along the banks of the Flint River. On the other side of the Flint River was a thirty-two-acre plot of pasture lands. At its southern end, near to Stapleton, was another fifteen acres of coffee and a ten-acre plantain walk. Mrs Turner, losing a husband and a son on the same day, perhaps did not wish to cope with estate management at Smailfield, and by 1806 had sold out.

William Burrowes faded from the official records, perhaps through death, in 1799. According to the map of Smailfield above, in 1806 Mrs Burrowes, who must be his widow, was the owner of Rock Spring Estate. Edward Marchant Burrowes, perhaps their heir, died in 1812. It is a Mrs P.E. Burrowes who consistently turned in reports to the Vestry concerning the estate after 1821. This suggests that widow Burrowes was not only owner but also resident manager of Rock Spring. An S.J. Burrowes appears consistently too, as the owner of some slaves. Was this the sister who mourned Edward Marchant's passing with such a glowing tribute? S.J. Burrowes's 1820 slave return was signed by E.M. Burrowes, an agent.[32] Another Edward Marchant in the family? And had S.J. left Rock Spring, with Mrs P.E., the sole female entrepreneur there between the beginning of the nineteenth century and full emancipation of the non-white population? What we do know, is that Mrs P.E. was active enough to go off, in 1817, to the United States of America accompanied by two of her mulatto slaves, returning by 1820.

Louisiana Estate in most of its retrieved Vestry returns – for 1824, 1826 and 1832 – is listed as the property of Peter and Louisa Burnett. According to the oral reports, Louisa is Peter's wife and the estate is named for her. The retrievable estate and crop accounts for this property, were never, as in the case of Mrs Jane Neilson, signed by Louisa, but they were never signed by Peter either. There is no way of knowing to what extent Louisa Burnett was involved in the management of Louisiana. Waterton was similarly listed as owned by a woman and a man – Elizabeth and John Rose Forbes. In its 1838 accounts we find the estate selling £5 3s. worth of coffee to a Mrs Forbes.[33] Hardly Elizabeth, the part owner! The reference does establish, however, that Forbes women were involved in business transactions in this pre-emancipation era. They continued to be so involved until 1840, at least as far as ownership is concerned, for in that year it was Elizabeth and Isabella who were now listed as owners of Waterton.

Then there was Mrs Bayliss, the wife of the Baptist minister who had worked among the flock at Brae Head in greater Woodside, whose Port Maria church had been burned down and who died in 1837. According to the news sent in 1837 to the *Baptist Missionary Herald,* the Baptists' journal, the widow had taken over some of the tasks formerly assigned to her husband and was doing well.[34]

Lucille Mathurin, writing about white women in Jamaica between 1655 and 1844, says of them in her PhD thesis, "A Historical Study of Women in Jamaica 1655–1844", they "came, saw and fled".[35] Lady Nugent in her journal supports this position for the first decade of the nineteenth century: she notes the absence of white women here. Hopewell was one of the estates she visited, and it must have been part of her database.[36] We have found no evidence of a woman owner or manager at this estate from which area children came to Woodside School in the twentieth century. The same can be said for Palmetto Grove, which, like Hopewell, was a sugar estate. The same cannot be positively said for the coffee estates of greater Woodside – Rock Spring, Smailfield, Waterton, Louisiana and Woodside proper. Here there were resident women likely to be white, and they were well represented in the field of business. There were also female owners on the periphery of greater Woodside. There was Patience Hermit who owned what sounds like the present Pear Tree Grove; Elizabeth Timberlake of Pleasant Hill, near to Stapleton; Mary Parker,[37] patentee of land close to Hazard, Change Hill and John Neilson's land; Margaret Neilson of Dunkeld; and others. These Woodside women were, however, like the others in Jamaica, in that they were not at all represented in the Vestry and the professions, though we do see the wife of a minister of religion standing in for her dead mate.[38]

The Socio-Economic Environment

The large acreages of land which came into the hands of Lord Bathurst and the Parkers had been, by 1804, made into estates ranging in size from Hopewell's eighteen hundred acres to Rock Spring's one hundred. Sugar cane had been the attraction in Jamaica in the eighteenth century. Perhaps planters throughout greater Woodside had turned to this. The crop accounts and detailed maps for this area mention sugar for Hopewell and Palmetto Grove only. Coffee, ground provisions, plantains and cows are the main attractions after 1804. This area was well suited to the production of coffee and the rearing of cattle. There were and still are several rivers in the area; they served as watering holes for cattle and as wash tubs for coffee and power for the coffee mills. Some were forded by bridges to allow movement between the estates' works and their fields. Sloping hills offered the drainage which coffee needs.

Greater Woodside's coffee men, penkeepers and sugar planters were pulled together into a closely knit unit by their service in the militia and in the Vestry. They called on each other for support – the agreement between William Neilson and Frances Maidstone Neilson, that the former should care for her son's estate until his majority, was witnessed by neighbour Harrison;[39] Frances Maidstone's attorney through whom she sold a slave in 1809 while she was in England, was R.R. Parker, presumably one of the Parkers of the greater Woodside area;[40] Peter Burnett, Mordecai Hart and William Walker came across to the Woodside great house to witness William John's will.[41] They were there at each other's weddings. They also did business with each other: William Neilson and Jonathan Forbes were in a business deal with William Pollock in 1804, with respect to land in Portland;[42] William Peterswold sold land to William John Neilson and evidently had lent money to the

Wrights,[43] the former owner of the land sold to Neilson; and Frances Neilson sold a slave to Mr William Parker.[44] They were consultants to each other: an R.R. Parker was Frances Neilson's lawyer;[45] John Crossman took charge of Smailfield and several other properties in the area.[46]

The Woodside area was, at this time, supplied with medical personnel, lawyers, surveyors and, it would seem, given the movement of properties to and from Crossman, with financiers. There were people such as McCrae who owned several slaves and little landed property;[47] it is a fair conclusion that these people supplied and hired slaves to their neighbours. Many of their transactions, the sale of a slave between neighbours for instance, were subject to the process of the law. Surveyors were kept busy as land sales were ratified by law; wills were registered, and even the withdrawal of an executor was done legally. Estates did not grow like Topsy but were well conceived and laid out, and in several cases, the kind of data kept on the property was such that allowed detailed crop accounts and returns to be submitted to the agencies of the government.

The white-owned properties of greater Woodside of the early nineteenth century look, from these data, like organized units, related to other organized units under the law. The resulting community reads like a cell. The community was not, however, a self-contained entity cut off from the rest of Jamaica and the world. People found mates from elsewhere, sold their products to other parts of Jamaica and to areas outside of Jamaica, visited England and the United States. Nor was the community of white property owners self-sufficient. Enslaved labour, of people distinguishable by physical features, powered it from below. Law and custom kept this "labour" in place. Like an anthill when it is opened or a boil when lanced, this "labour" erupted with emancipation into individual human beings, each guided by his or her own concerns. The units and the cell felt it. The eruption was too much for Mrs Jane Neilson: she lost her head, it seems.

Chapter 4

Blacks among the Whites in Greater Woodside, 1799–1838

The black people of Woodside, like the black people of Jamaica and the rest of the New World, came here from Africa principally to serve white people from Europe, such as those presented in the last section. The people from Europe came to Jamaica, for the most part, voluntarily. They came in search of wealth with which to improve their status in Britain. Simon Taylor, the richest man in Jamaica in his day and the owner of, among other estates, Flint River Estate and Pen in St Mary, Jamaica, had it as his aim to make his nephew, Sir Simon Taylor, the richest commoner in England.[1] So preoccupied were these migrants with Britain and the life there, that they named areas here after areas there. Thus, close to Woodside were Highgate, Hampstead, Richmond, Islington, places contiguous or close to each other in England. These names existed in other parishes in Jamaica as well. Richmond, Highgate and Woodside appear in the parish of Manchester.

Those black people who came here between 1611, the year of the first recorded census, and 1807, the year when the importation of Africans as slaves legally ended in British territories, were, unlike the Europeans – Spanish at first, English after – not part of the decision to move from the place of their birth to another country. They were brought here in chains and without knowing where they were being taken and why, and while here in Jamaica were completely under the jurisdiction of their masters. They were chattel slaves, and so were their children and their descendants, for this status was inherited and could not be officially changed solely by their own efforts. Official freedom was the gift of the master.

There were other people besides the African who were subordinate to the white landowners in Woodside and elsewhere in the New World, though only the African slave inherited his subordination. There were whites who were employed to white landowners; there were whites who were too poor to qualify for the vote or to get commissions in the military. These would not have been invited to the socials of the wealthier whites, would not have been at table with Governor and Lady Nugent as they dined at Hopewell. But such subordination was social, not biological, and could end when the necessary wealth was acquired.

There were also black people who were no longer bound to serve anyone but could choose for whom they worked. Their new status had to be determined by law and with the cooperation of their masters, who would have had to sign manumission agreements. Another free group of non-whites were persons born out of the relationship between enslaved black women and their white masters; called coloureds, they were often manumitted by their fathers. Some of these freed persons even became landowners: the historian Swithin Wilmot tells us that many of the coffee planters in St Thomas-in-the-Vale, the parish in which most of Louisiana and Pear Tree Grove were located, were coloureds.[2] But the fact that they were now legally bound to no other individual and did own property did not mean that they were equal to whites, for unlike the whites moving from poverty to wealth, the number of acres coloureds were permitted to own was limited, and so was their access to the vote and to representation in the House of Assembly.

The records concerning births, burials and baptisms give some information on these non-white free people. But while they do give the colour of a person as well as his or her legal status, they do not consistently give the addresses of these people. The records are also limited in that they pertain only to baptismal and burial rites performed by the Church of England. Assuming that free black and coloured people held no strong prejudices against the Church of England, and vice versa, the records do allow us to say that the number of free coloureds baptized in St Mary in the period before emancipation was relatively small, and that few carry the surnames of the estate owners discussed in the preceding chapter. In the records a birth is listed not *of* but *to* a Neilson who is a mulatto, and she produces a child who is registered in 1826 as Jane Walker:[3] a Neilson might have made this mulatto mother. Among the baptisms, there is Rebecca Peterswold (*sic*) of Petersfield, baptized in 1817.[4] "Peterswald" and "Peterswold" are interchangeable in the records: Neilson and Peterswa(o)ld are surnames familiar in greater Woodside and its environs. These cases notwithstanding, it does seem that whites and the blacks in the Woodside area were able to keep their relationship as apart socially and sexually as it was legally. Such behaviour would be consonant with the existence of resident white women in the greater Woodside area and its environs, a matter already discussed.

Inherited racial subordination such as that experienced by blacks in Woodside and Jamaica was peculiar to the New World, for in some other places where slavery was practised, social mobility was possible. It even happened that people who had previously been introduced into the society as slaves, became part of the royal house there, and possible too in some such societies for a slave to be freed and to immediately become part of the upper class. The Euro-American anthropologists Kopytoff and Meirs offer us an example:

> The great grandfather of the Russian poet Pushkin was an African slave acquired in France by Peter the Great who ordered his marriage into a Russian noble family – a clear instance of sponsorship on social placement. In the New World, however, almost all slaves entered the society as chattels of private persons, and further formal limitations on their mobility were imposed by society at large on the basis of race.[5]

This kind of social mobility depends on the point at which people come into the system of slavery and on the intentions of those who induct them into the system. Woodside's slaves, as slaves of the New World, came into this system as chattel owned by private people. These people wanted them for manual labour and for nothing else: not to be scribes or tutors of their children. Occupational mobility outside of manual estate labour was inconceivable in this situation.

What did these subordinated persons do in Woodside? They watched the men of the Forbes family moving down from Waterton to collect the Neilsons and together make their way to Rock Spring and Smailfield, where they collect the Turners and Burrowes and set off for Hopewell, where they meet the Pollocks at the Grant house, there to meet visiting dignitaries such as Governor Nugent and his wife, who visited on 23

March 1802.[6] They would have watched these white men, as, dressed in their flaming red coats, the military uniform of the time, they paraded, drilled and were reviewed. Some of them might actually be in the party, seeing to their masters' clothes, currying their horses, and might even have been with them on the parade ground, carrying their firelocks and halberts, the military weapons used then, as observed elsewhere in Jamaica by Lady Nugent.[7]

Black people must have served at the weddings and the parties, and certainly related with white families as cooks and washerwomen and as workmen seeing to coffee, cattle and other parts of the estate economy. They watched and perhaps accompanied their masters, many of whom were Quakers, to meetings of the Society of Friends. They watched their masters. Was this guest, Farquaharson, here to make arrangements for shipping a house to his estate in St Elizabeth, as happened in 1828?[8] Farquaharson according to the slave registers, had a large number of slaves, most of whom bore his name; no landed property is mentioned until years later.[9] Farquaharson seems to have been involved initially in the internal slave trade, satisfying the needs of his parishioners in St Mary. The enslaved community might ask on seeing him: is he here to interest the master in his collection of slaves? Why has surveyor Walker ridden down from Carron Hall? Was the master about to sell off another bit of land?

The black/white relationship in the greater Woodside area, as in Jamaica as a whole, was to some extent like two intertwined circles, a common arc of close relationships with parts totally black and parts totally white. In the smaller plantation houses, according to Lady Nugent, blacks sometimes slept on the floor in the master's house;[10] children under six ran about the house like pets. At Hopewell on her 1802 visit, Lady Nugent's mule was left in the hands of a "parcel of blacks". She dined at six o'clock with a large party of gentlemen and met "mulatto(s)", several of whom gave her "their histories".[11] They represented the ultimate expression of the intertwining: "They are all daughters of Members of the Assembly and officers, etc etc."[12] On her journey to Hopewell, Lady Nugent stopped at Montpellier Estate and at Bath. She stopped at Golden Grove, at the Moro and at Merton, all in the east end of the island. It was only at Mr Bryan's estate at Port Antonio that she met a white woman: "Mrs Cosens is the first white woman, except my maid, that I have seen since we began our journey".[13]

A white housekeeper was a rarity, according to Lady Nugent's researches: instead of white women, a bevy of yellow, brown and black women, slave or free, were in the houses interacting with the men of all statuses.

The rest of greater Woodside does not accord with this picture of Hopewell. On these coffee-growing estates there were quite a number of white women. There were women as wives and owners of property – Forbes women, Neilson women, Pollocks, Turners; and there were women guests at weddings kept in Woodside and neighbouring Carron Hall – the Pupleys, the MacKays, Crossmans – enough for a socio-sexual life and enough to confine interracial relations to the work scene. Marriage, as we shall later see, was an option exercised by slaves in this area. This exercise needed the blessing of the white estate-owner and speaks, it seems, of a culture less sexually licentious than might have been the case on Hopewell Estate as suggested by Lady Nugent's narrative.

The lists in table 4.1 show the numbers of enslaved persons in the greater Woodside area and the estates to which they were attached.

Table 4.1   Number of Enslaved Persons in the Greater Woodside Area, 1811–1832

	1811	1821	1824	1826	1832
Change Hill	173	21	–	–	–
Windsor Castle	169	–	39	335 (with Decoy)	–
Hopewell	414	416	417 (Pen and Estate)	417	418
Flemington	1	2	–	–	–
Braemar	1	–	46	–	–
Palmetto Grove	243	261	327 (Grove and Pen)	–	223
Louisiana	–	119	125	131	135
Rock Spring	–	54	45	44	50
Waterton	–	28	39	41	–
Woodside	153	162	173	184	162
Smailfield	–	–	74	71	63
Richmond Hill	–	–		39	–
Total	1,001	942	1,596	1,223	1,051

Source: Derived from the *Jamaica Almanack*, 1811–1840.

Where there are spaces in the table above, no returns were made to the Vestry for that year for that estate. If we assume negligence rather than a closure of the estates, we would have to conclude that in the years 1811–32 there was an annual average of about one thousand enslaved persons in the Woodside area.

Some of these persons might have been born in Jamaica and even born of parents who were born in Jamaica. They would have been quite accustomed to Jamaican life and to their place in it. The slave trade ended in 1807: some might therefore have been born in Africa and would be still unfamiliar with the life of slavery, still having memories of Africa, still selecting by reflex African frames of reference, still listening for their names. The information we have on a large estate like Hopewell for the years 1817 and 1820 indicates that in the earlier of these two periods,[14] of the 415 slaves on that estate, 305 were native-born and 110 were African-born, the latter being in excess of 25 per cent of the total number of slaves. The figure was less in 1820. Of 416 enslaved persons at Hopewell, 326 were native-born and only 90 were African-born, the latter being now a percentage of about twenty-one. These 110 people and 90 people, the latter no doubt part of the former, must have left Africa with names, and would have been old enough to know what those names were. Where were those names? Throughout Jamaica they disappeared into ones reflecting the perception the masters had of them – Congo Jack, Chamba Jack; into the names of Greek and Roman figures – Cato, Mercury, Nero, Jupiter, Cupid, Venus, as seen in the slave returns for Dr Neilson's Woodside Estate of 1817 and 1820, reproduced in table 4.2a and 4.2b.[15] Other greater Woodside estates had their share of Greek and Roman namesakes, especially Cato and Cupid.

Table 4.2a The Enslaved on Dr William J. Neilson's Woodside Estate (Woodside Proper), 1817

*Jacob alias John Neilson	Mulatto	40	American
Buton(?) alias John Cunningham	Negro	6	African
Bouney	''	60	''
Carson	''	60	''
Charles alias John Graham	''	55	''
Garrick alias John Garrick	''	55	''
Howe	''	55	''
Jacob	''	50	''
Duke alias Philip Johnson	''	50	''
Moses alias Hugh Walker	''	45	''
England alias James Neilson	''	50	''
Andrew alias William Bonshe	''	45	''
Sharper alias James Patterson	''	40	''
Tom alias Peter Burnett	''	45	''
Will alias George Russel	''	32	''
Sam	''	35	''
Byndloss alias Prince Logan	''	32	''
Albert alias Bob Cunningham	''	35	''
Grenville alias Tom Smith	''	30	''
Romeo alias John Minott	''	30	''
Essex alias Lawrence Neilson	''	20	''
Kent	''	30	''
Bob alias Jonathan Forbes	''	5	''
Walter alias Alexander Binnings	''	26	''
Ferdinand alias Harry Bailey	''	28	''
John alias John McCrea	''	35	''
Collingwood alias Thomas Collingwood	''	2	''
Nelson alias Robert Nelson	''	22	''
Andrew alias Andrew Alston	Mulatto	20	Creole
William alias Bob Duncan	Negro	35	''
Russel alias Charles Green	''	30	''
Dick alias Edward White	''	25	''
*Billy alias Angus Morrison	''	40	''

Table 4.2a continued

Dennis alias William Parker	Negro	35	Creole	
Frederck alias Robert Nelson	''	30	''	
Sammy	''	26	''	
Polidor alias William Johnson	''	35	''	
John Brown alias George Thelwell	''	18	''	
Peter	''	10	''	
*Garrick alias Richard Walker	''	16	''	
King alias Billy Miller	''	40	''	
Frank alias William Francis	''	40	''	son of Christmas
Hector alias Charles Beckford	''	35	''	''
*Cato alias Edward Beckford	''	30	''	''
Nero alias Richard Baxter	''	28	''	''
Jupiter alias George Wellington	''	30	''	son of Nancy
*England alias Thomas Downs	''	28	''	''
Cuffee alias Alick Donaldson	''	26	''	''
Othello alias Thomas Walker	''	18	''	''
Mercury alias James Kelly	''	20	''	son of Lizzy
*Sandy alias William Cosen	''	26	''	''
Simon alias April Black	''	18	''	''
*Quamin alias William Ferguson	''	30	''	son of Charlotte
Cupid alias Thomas Newry	''	25	''	''
Hunter(?) alias Richard Parker	''	40	''	son of Betty
*Monday alias Donald Patterson	''	35	''	son of Dolly
Edinburgh alias Lewis Kelly	''	18	''	son of Barbary
Godfrey alias Lewis Kelly	''	10	''	son of Patty
Jeffry alias Lewis Kelly	''	10	''	son of Belfry Barrett
Scotland alias Bob Johnson	''	8	''	son of Rosaline Green
Cason alias Richard Green	''	3	''	''
Harry alias Charles Smith	''	8	''	son of Laura
Lewis/Levi(?)	''	3	''	''
Allick alias Walter Brown	''	8	''	son of Kitty Brown
Derry	''	3	''	son of Martilla
*Edward John Marshall	''	4	''	son of Mary Ann Drew

Table 4.2a *continued*

*Quaco alias Tom Downs	Negro	1	Creole	son of Charlotte Downs
John Bull alias Allick Rennalls	Sambo	10	''	son of Cecilia Williams
Edward	''	4	''	son of Mary Neilson
John	''	2	''	''
*Thomas Howard	''	50	runaway	
Betty	Negro	80	African	
Dotty	''	75	''	
Penny(?)	''	60	''	
Christmas	''	70	''	
Delia	''	60	''	
Sally	''	55	''	
Charlotte	''	55	''	
Lucy alias Lizz Williams	''	55	''	
Barbary	''	55	''	
Chloe alias Venus Neilson	''	50	''	
Juliet alias Jenny/Terry(?) Duff	''	50	''	
Kathy alias Adaline Lewis	''	50	''	
Flora	''	50	''	
Nancy	''	60	''	
Peggy alias Mary(?) Neilson	''	50	''	
Damsel alias Bessy Barrett	''	48	''	
Bella alias Jane Walker	''	48	''	
*Belinda alias Fidelia Morrison	''	35	''	
Louisa Brown	''	35	''	
Lucretia alias Rosaline Green	''	30	''	
Quiano(?) alias Charlotte Downs	''	30	''	
Laura	''	28	''	
Nora	''	28	''	
Leah alias Susannah Russel	''	28	''	
Clara alias Sophy Cunningham	''	28	''	
Louisa alias Caroline Maorse(?)	''	25	''	
Fanny alias Mary Ann Drew	''	23	''	
Patty	''	35	''	

Table 4.2a continued

Ann Phillips	Mulatto	40	Creole	
Abigail Jones	Negro	60	''	
Harriat alias Geogiana Needham	''	40	''	
Esther alias Jearnet Neilson	''	30	''	
Tema alias Cornelia Neilson	''	30	''	
Juliet alias Mary Neilson	''	33	''	
Eve	''	32	''	
Angela alias Lente Patterson	''	20	''	
Bessy alias Becky Neilson	''	35	''	
*Rachel alias Isabel Bel	''	22	''	
Charity alias Isabella Patterson	''	10	''	
Daphne alias Nancy Patterson	''	10	''	
Evelina alias Julian Richard	''	10	''	daughter of Bessy Barrett
Molly alias Fanny Beckford	''	25	''	''
Rosette	''	22	''	''
Katherine alias Cornelia Ales	''	16	''	''
Seilly (Sally?) alias Becky Francis	''	12	''	''
Clarissa alias Ann McKenzie	''	22	''	daughter of Margaret Neilson
*Selina Montague	Sambo	20	''	''
*Celestine Neilson	''	16	''	''
*Justina Neilson	''	16	''	''
Pamela Cunningham	Negro	14	''	''
Cecilly alias Kitty	''	35	''	daughter of Sally
Maria alias Mary Parker	''	32	''	''
Martilla	''	28	''	''
Rachel alias Cecilia Williams	''	33	''	daughter of Charlotte
Sukey alias Sarah Williams	''	22	''	''
Susanna alias Dorothy Patterson	''	33	''	daughter of Nancy
Lettuce alias Elizabeth Francis	''	22	''	''
Olive alias Amelia Burnett	''	18	''	daughter of Jene Walker
Rosy alias Agnes Thomas	''	12	''	daughter of Jean Walker

Table 4.2a continued

Phibby alias Sophia Patterson	Negro	9	Creole	daughter of Jean Walker
*Cathery(?) alias Henrietta Morrison	"	14	"	daughter of Fidelia Morrison
*Princess alias Love Morrison	"	3	"	"
Cretia alias Jean Thomas Brown	"	12	"	daughter of Kitty
Jenny alias Elsie Thomas	"	9	"	"
Marina alias Susan Russel	"	9	"	daughter of Mary Ann Parker
Diana	"	7	"	daughter of Martilla
Charlotte	"	16	"	daughter of Cecilia Williams
Mary alias Marina Rennals	Sambo	7	"	"
Jane	"	3	"	"
Elizabeth White	Negro	6	"	daughter of Fanny Beckford
Lydia alias Rosanna Beckford	"	1	"	"
Louisa alias Letitia Russell	"	6	"	daughter of Charlotte Downs
Joan	"	6	"	daughter of Nora
Betty	"	1	"	daughter of Rosetta
Elinor Patterson	Mulatto	10	"	daughter of Jennet Neilson
Mary Ann Patterson	"	7	"	"
Caroline Needham	Negro	6 mos.	"	daughter of Georgiana Needham
*Queen	"	1	"	daughter of Selina Montague

Males = 72

Females = 78

Total = 150

28 June 1817

Source: Register of Slave Returns (St Mary) 1B/11/7/62, Jamaica Archives, 28 June 1817

Table **4.2b** The Enslaved on Dr William J. Neilson's Woodside Estate (Woodside Proper), 1820

Name	Colour	Age	Origin	Parentage	Event
*Billy Ferguson	Negro	3	Creole	son of Mary Ann Drew	birth
Mansfield Smith	"	3	"	son of Laura alias Johanna Smith	"
Charles	"	3	"	son of Seante Patterson	"
Bonny(?)	"	3	"	son of Nora	"
Douglass	"	38	"		death
*Wm Ferguson	"	33	"		death
*John Neilson	Mulatto	43	African		death
Carson	Negro	63	"		sold to Andrew Heron(?) Kingston
Lydia	"	3	Creole	daughter of Nora birth	
Alfee(?)	"	3	"	daughter of Myrtilla	"
Lavinia	"	3	"	daughter of of Cecilia Williams	"
Chance	"	3	"	daughter of Eve	"
*Margaret Conohie	Mulatto	3	"	daughter of Isabella Bele	birth ("manumized" July 1820)
Peggy	Sambo	2	"	daughter of Mary Neilson	birth
*Nadalina Frances Walker	Negro	1½	"	daughter of Selina Montague	"
Penelope	"	1	"	daughter of Celestina Neilson	"
Princess	"	1	"	daughter of Fanny Beckford	"
Salay(?) Richards	"	1	"	daughter of Evelina Richard	"
*Prudence	"	1	"	daughter of Charlotte Downs	"
Dolly	"	2 mos	"	daughter of Sophie Cunningham	"
Betty	"	80	African		death
Dolly	"	70	"		"

Source: Register of Slave Returns (St Mary) 1B/11/7/42, Jamaica Archives.

The 1820 list contains seventeen names, but only nine persons are added to the 150 total of 1817, for death, manumission and sale have taken away some. This entry has, with respect to William John Neilson, beside the usual "do swear", the words "or if a Quaker do solemnly affirm".

In 1817, when the registration of slaves became mandatory, only three enslaved persons on Dr Neilson's plantation had African names that were taken seriously enough to be entered into the public records. One was Quamin, one was Quaco and the other was Cuffee, West African (Akan) day names. All were creoles. The African-born – fifty-four persons, or a bit more than one third of the labour force – had English names, even names of British places such as Essex, Kent, England, Edinburgh, Scotland. No woman had an African name except possibly Charlotte Downs, who could be Quiano – the writing is not clear – and who was born in Africa, was only thirty, and might have come to Jamaica with, and remembered, her name. What of the other young African women on the Woodside proper estate – Leah alias Susanna Russell, Clara alias Sophy Cunningham and Louisa alias Caroline Maorise(?) all aged twenty-eight, and Fanny alias Mary Ann Drew, aged twenty-three? Where were their African names? Charlotte Downs at least remembers to name her child Quaco. The same pattern was seen on other greater Woodside estates – a poor showing of African names.

It can be assumed that enslaved persons, like other people, were emotionally tied to their native land and would have wanted to hand down traditional names to their children, as was the custom at home. Dolly made an attempt to keep the African concept of day names: her child was named Monday. But only three women, as already mentioned, actually managed to give their children African names that stuck; none of the women was allowed to keep her name officially. These women were named Dolly, Damsel, Christmas and so on; the sons they made were Scotland, John Bull, Othello, Mercury, Jupiter, Nero, Cato, Hector, Cupid and other epic characters; their daughters were Rachel, Katherine and other European names.

Where did the natural and learned desire to pass on and keep traditional names go? Into the registry of the oral tradition. Where the powerful people in your most significant setting call you, and frequently, by a special name, it sticks and is remembered. The name the master gives, used frequently in the work setting by the overseer in the field or the mistress in the house, is the name likely to stay with you and to become socially accepted. The African name that you brought with you or that was given you by your parents, remained registered in the private memory and was relatively quickly forgotten. A new name sealed a new identity. There is no peep of an African name or concept of naming in Dr Neilson's slave returns after 1817, for the years 1823, 1826 and 1829, or in his wife's returns for 1832.

Some enslaved people had just one name and their children were described as "daughter of . . .", "son of . . ." – always "of" their mother. On some estates they had an alias, two names. The African-born twenty-year-old Essex, for instance, had the alias, "Lawrence Neilson". The African-born thirty-year-old Romeo had the alias "John Minott". These aliases seemed to have been names given at baptism. This means that Essex and Romeo knew themselves by three different sets of names – the names by which they were called in Africa, the names their masters gave them, and the names they took at baptism and which were now registered officially in the government's records and the church registers. A new situation, a new name. Their life in Christendom now begins. Their official history begins; this is primarily how they will be called as ancestors. The names of those ancestors of the people of greater Woodside, whose official identity came to them through the Anglican baptism, are below by plantation.

Change Hill (1817 and 1818)

James Abrahams	Daniel Allen	Francis Allen
Nellie Anderson**	Polly Anderson**	John Barnaby
Robert Bennet	Richard Brien	Thomas Brien
Charles Brown	William Campbell**	Nelson Crossman*
Olive Crossman*	Thomas Davis	George Duncan
Margaret Edwards	Thomas Gordon	John Green
Joseph Green	John Hart*	Rosey Hart*
Parchenia Harris	Annie Harrison*	Davy Harrison*
Henry Harrison*	Hibbert Harrison*	Nugent Harrison*
Princess Harrison*	Robert Harrison*	Rodney Harrison*
Tom Harrison*	Thomas Henry	Saunders Hibbert
Beatrice Johnson	James Lewin	Henry Lindsay

Harriot Lynch	Robert Lynch	Primus Mitchell
Diana Morgan	Ann Murphy	Nanny Pameo
William Patrick	Margaret Richards	Elizabeth Roberts
Priscilla Rowley	Christian Thomas	Rosanna Thomas
Lewis Thompson	Beckford Walters	Eleanor Walters
Charles Williams**	Gracey Williams**	

Hopewell (1820–1833)

Joe Agilwe	Thomas Anderson	Lasanna Anslin
Susanna Bassifte	Andrew Black	James Brice
Minna Brice	Olvida Brice	Bessy Brown
Dixon Newgent Brown	Jenny Brown	
Kitty Francis Brown	Lewis Brown	
Patrick Brown	Robert Brown	Tom Brown
Ann Browne	Sam Burrel	Cecelia Campbell**
John Campbell**	Thomas Campbell**	James Grant Clark**
Hannah Ann Clark**	Hughina Clarke**	Letitia Clarke**
Nancy Clarke**	Nanny Collingridge	Milly Ann Coutrice
Agnes Davis	Bella Davis	Lydia Davis
Susannah Dawee	John Dobson	Rianna Dobson
Sally Doraine	Catharine Douce	Charles Douglas
Edward Douglas	Margaret Douglas	Mary Douglas
Ruth Douglas	Thomas Walton Douglas	
Tom Douglas	James Dury	Baptis Edwards**
Barbara Edwards**	Lenona Edwards**	Mary Ann Edwards**
William Edwards**	Lucy Ennis	Joseph Forbes**
Nancy Forret	John Francis	Biddy Fraser
Caroline Fraser	John Fraser	Robert Fraser
Thomas Gayle	Charles Gordon	Hercules Gordon
Jessy Ann Gordon	Mary Ann Gordon	Sally Gordon
Licet Johnston Gordon	Frances Graham	
Alexander Grant*	Bihemy Grant*	Charles C. Grant*
Entie Grant*	Estina Grant*	Flora Grant*

George Grant*	Henora Grant*	James Barry Grant*
Job Grant*	Julia Ann Grant*	Lewis Grant*
Melina Grant*	Peachy Grant*	Thomas Grant**
Christiana Green	Diana Green	Edward Green
Richard Green	Jane Hackett	George Hamilton
Nancy Hamilton	Thomas Hamilton	William Hamilton
Biddy Harris	Charles Harris	George Harris
James Harris	Patrenie Harrie	William Morris Harris
Billy Henry	Sarah Anne Hodgeson	Fanny Hudson
James Hornsby Hudson	Joseph Hudson	Latina Hudson
Louisa Hudson	Mary Hudson	Punie Richard Hudson
Ben Hynes	Alick Jackson	Pussley Jackson
Theresa Jackson	Ava Arabella Johnson	
Maggie Johnson	Eliza Lewis Johnson	
Lilly Johnston	George Kean	Lewis Kelly
Lucinda Kerr	James Miller Kerridge	
Nancy Kerridge	Roseanne Kerridge	Diana Leslie**
Harriot Leslie**	Thomas Alden Leslie**	
Ann-Maria Lewis	Maria Lewis	Henry Lipscomb
Elsie Machison	Elizabeth Matthewson	
Alexander McBean	George McLeod	Nancy McNabb
David Miller	Joseph Montague	George Neilson**
Belinda Nugent	Charles Thomas Nugent	
George Myers Nugent	William Pite(?)	Walter Pollock**
William Raden	Charles Redwood**	Peter Reid
Robert Reid	Penelope Ross	James Russell
William Simpson	Mary Ann Sims	Mary Sinclair
Beckford Speight	Henry Speight	Marcia Speight
Ellen Spink	John Stevens	Caroline Susan
Fredrick Tharp	Lizzey Thomas	Patty Eliza Thomas
Henry Lewis Thompson	Patrick Thompson	
Isabella Turner**	Robert Turner**	
Joseph Augustus Watson	George Wellington	
Patrick Wilson	Alick Wright	Samuel Yates

Louisiana (1824–1834)

Abraham Alexander (sambo)	Charles Battice	
Jack Burnett (sambo)*	John Burnett (sambo)*	
Henrietta Deans**	Daniel Grant**	
James Hamilton (sambo)	Eliza James (sambo)	
Lucretia McDermott	Alexander Nelson	Fanny Nelson
Dolly Parker**	Patty Parker**	Edward Rennales
James Stanbury (sambo)	Jimmy Stanbury	
Sophia Stanbury	William Stanbury	
James Stewart	Lewis Stewart	
Letitia Stewart (sambo)	Mary Thomas	

Palmetto Grove (1818–1831)

Mary Aitkin	Alexander Harper Anderson**	
Ann-Elizabeth Anderson**	Eliza Anderson**	Charles Bellet
Abraham Bennet	Thomas Billet	Eleanor Brown
Molly Clark**	Mary Clarke** (quadroon)	
James Deans*	James Edwards**	Jane Forrester
John Forrester	Thomas Gowan	Bella Henry
Richard Henry	Bessy Issard	Sarah Issard
Maria Johnston	Jacob Lee	Robert Longron
Bob Markland	Dick Richards	John Richards
Isaac Roberts	Liddy Roberts	Mary Russell
Neptune Shaw	Ann Simpson	Bridget Simpson
Janet Sterling	Becky Taylor**	Oxford Thaw
Margaret Ann Thomas	Aphelia Thompson	
Isaac Walker**	Dolly Wharam	John White
Amelia Williams**	Phillis Williams**	Charles Wright*

Petersfield (1817–1831)

Janet Bolt	Rachael Welsh Bolt	Edward Burnett**
Nelly Burnet**	Peter Burnet**	Sinola Burnet**

Emily Byfield

Catherine Cook

Clarilsa Crosby

John Cyrus

Henry Dakes

Membra Dido

Charles Edwards**

Ann Flannagan

Ned Ford

Catharine Frances

Diana Frances

December Hibbert

James Hibbert

Sandy Hibbert

Margaret Jenkins

Clarinda Macrea**

Dennis Macrea**

Lavinia Macrea**

Lucindo Macrea**

Billy McDonald**

Lewis McDonald**

Sally McDonald**

Myrtilla McDonald**

Sandy McGregor

Deborah Meyers

Caroline Mitchell

Amelia Mitchell

George Pennington

Grace Peters

John Peters

Sally Peters

Elizabeth Read

Elizabeth Redwood**

Mary Ann Smith

James Stanton

Joe Thomas

Charles White

Mary White

Richard White

Rebecca Whittle

Guy Williams**

Margaret Williams**

Phillis Williams**

Mary Williamson

Deborah Zwire/Swire

Jane Zwire/Swire

Maria Zwire/Swire

Richmond Hill (1817–1834)

Agnes Hamilton

Charles Hamilton

George Hamilton

Lynch Hamilton

Lettice Hamilton

Tanny Hamilton

Godfrey Johnston

Philip Johnston

Alexander Patterson*

Barbary Patterson*

Richard Roper

Joseph Walker**

Rock Spring (1819–1831)

Thomas Cunningham**

Brian Rainsford

Cecilia Rainsford

Jasper Walker**

John Walker**

Phillis Walker**

Lavinia Walters

Smailfield

No listing seen in the records

Stapleton (1825–1830)

Joseph Buchanan**

Archibald Duncan

Mitchell Timberlake**

Isabella White

Waterton

No listing seen in the records

Woodside (1817–1831)

Dalton Bryan	Eliza Carie	Joseph Chambers
James Conie	Robert Conie	Christina Donaldson
Jeminy Donaldson	John Donaldson	Morgiana Downs
George William Francis	Ann Forbes**	Frances Grandison
Isabella Grandison	John Grant**	Charlotte Hamilton
Joseph Hamilton	Peter Hamilton	Eleanor Hare
Jemima Henry	John Henry	Richard Henry
Charles Hermit**	Donald Hermit**	Rebecca James
William Kelly	Fama Lee	Margaret McConochie
Thomas Morrison	Edward Neilson*	Fanny Neilson*
John Neilson*	Cecilia Richards	Janet Richards
Jack Sinclair	Edwin Smith	Ethelinda Smith
Livingstone Smith	Sabina Thomas	Ann Taylor**
Marina Walker**	Selina Walker**	Wilhelmina Walker**
Conie Wilson	Diana Wilson	Hannah Williams**
Jacket Hermitt**	James Campbell	Elizabeth Johnson

Skin colour was an important marker in those days, as was one's legal status, so slave baptisms were registered in a place different from that of white and free persons. Occasionally, by virtue of being baptized on the same day and at the same place, free mulatto baptisms were registered along with that of the enslaved, but the colour or legal distinctions were clearly stated. This happened only in two cases – with Helen Cunningham and Rebecca Peterswold of Petersfield, who were baptized on 29 September 1817. On occasion too, the recorder of these baptisms saw fit to record the colour of the enslaved. This happened in six cases on the Louisiana estate. These persons were distinguished as "sambo". This happened in one case on the Palmetto Grove estate. The person to whom attention was being drawn in the latter case, was Mary Clarke, a quadroon. The sambo people on the Louisiana estate were James Stanbury, James Hamilton, Abraham Alexander, Letitia Thomas,

John Burnett and Jack Burnett. It seems fair to conclude, given the recorders' care in noting legal status and colour, that the remaining persons baptized into the Anglican faith were the black enslaved children and possibly adults. We know for certain with respect to the Woodside population that about a half of these ancestors were three years old and below in 1831, for some of the names of the baptized did not appear on any of the slave returns for the period 1817–29.

A review of the slave lists for the whole parish of St Mary shows that only a minority of enslaved people, like Lawrence Neilson, had the two-name combine associated with the British culture.[16] On such lists, as with that of Woodside proper, this two-name combine is entered as "alias". On a few, this style is referred to as "Christian name". This two-name combine is evidently related to baptism into the Christian faith. The same review of slave lists shows a significant number of last names to be that of the owner, even when the enslaved is listed as "African". About a third of Farquaharson's well over three hundred slaves on his Job's Hill Estate, for instance, have his surname. The same goes for Wright of the Palmetto Grove estate. We can infer from this that these enslaved people, possibly baptized en masse, were at the time of their baptism part of the property of the people whose names they took. The acclaimed 2001 British-made film *Gosford Park*, set in the social milieu of England's gentry, has one character advising an American valet travelling with his master, that all servants were called by their master's surname. To be given the name of your master seems to be part of British style which could have been transmitted to St Mary, Jamaica. Closer home, Mrs Burke of Treadways, St Catherine, in an interview in 1975, explained that in slavery days there were black Gyles and white Gyles, the former given this surname because, newly arrived from Africa, they could not communicate their names and were summarily given the names of their master. There could be a tradition of enslaved people being given their master's surnames.[17] In any case, it would also be very convenient for the general public to identify and refer to an enslaved person, socially a possession, by his master's name. That name was likely to be carried for life.

Where there is a surname which is not that of the master, it seems highly likely, then, that that person carried the name with him from an earlier situation, cementing it, possibly, with baptism. Accordingly, we assume that the enslaved in the lists above who share the surnames of their masters, and against whom we have put asterisks, were baptized while in the service of their current masters or were owned by no other master. The number is very small, an indication that a high proportion of the enslaved inhabitants of greater Woodside, most of whom were black-skinned, and excepting the very young who are with their mothers and whose origins are thus very clear, had a Jamaican past that preceded Woodside. The list too, according to our reasoning, indicates an inter-estate and intra–St Mary exchange. The double asterisk (**) singles out surnames that have been seen in the property lists in St Mary prior to 1840, or in the neighbouring districts in St Thomas-in-the-Vale, or have been seen on the 1804 map of greater Woodside and its environs. Some of these names – Forbes, Wright, Ferguson, Grant, Leslie, Neilson, Walker, Brown – are shared by surveyors who worked in St Mary and neighbouring St Catherine between 1780 and 1838.[18]

Orlando Patterson writes of the profligacy of estate owners and Lady Nugent, their contemporary, concurs; so we know that a similarity in names sometimes speaks of a sexual connection between slave and master.[19] We have seen above that among the baptized there were sambo slaves on Burnett's Louisiana Estate who have his name. A master-slave sexual connection could therefore have occurred on this greater Woodside estate to produce them; but, being sambo, this connection would have had to be a generation away. This is the sole case with respect to the group we are now calling "ancestors". The incidence of sexual connections that produce free coloureds is, from the evidence we have, also slight. The baptismal records do not give the district of residence of free persons: the lists pertain to parish. In addition, they do not always say whether the free persons baptized are coloured, the possible result of a master-slave union, or black. We also do not know how complete the baptismal list is with respect to free blacks and coloureds, for although we do know from Gad Heuman that free blacks and coloureds had to register,[20] we do not know whether baptismal records were their way of registering. What we can say is that very few of the persons designated as free and coloured in this list bear the names of estate owners living in the greater Woodside area.

We also know that with respect to Woodside Estate there was, between 1817 and 1820, slightly over 150 enslaved persons, only four of whom were mulatto, and nine of whom were sambo. Only one of these thirteen persons carried the name of the master. He was Jacob "alias John Neilson". He was forty years old in 1817, older than the master. He was listed as American-born, so that if he had been sired by the master's father, the conception did not take place in Woodside. A similar argument goes for the sambo twins on Dr Neilson's estate in 1817 who carry his name. They would have to have been made a generation away. In any case, since they were born when he was about ten years old, he is definitely cleared of a paternity charge. The other available slave returns for Dr Neilson's property – for the years 1823, 1826 and 1829 – carry two mulattos. They have the same mother and the same surname, and are the only evidence of a black/white sexual encounter in Woodside proper for this period. Their surname is not Neilson or that of any planter in the greater Woodside area discussed in the preceding chapters. We have to conclude, if our assumptions about naming are correct, that there was either very little profligacy here or very little issue of profligacy in this area, and that several older slaves had served with masters other than those of the greater Woodside area.

The relevant question posed by the names of the older enslaved, then, is not one of genetic attachment but of ownership: at what time was Jenny Forbes, part of the owned labour force of the Forbes of Waterton, Donnington Castle or Hamwalk, moved to Petersfield? Why was Charles Redwood sold away from the Redwood properties of Redwood Penn, June Walk or Philipsburg, into the Hopewell community of enslaved persons?[21] Our conclusion, based on this understanding, is that few of the enslaved persons in the greater Woodside area between 1817 and 1829 began their history here. They were probably parts of bloodlines and social networks that extended throughout Jamaica.

Bloodlines are dear to everyone. In slave society in Jamaica, mating couples did not necessarily live together: paternity could, therefore, not be easily assumed. In most cultures surnames signify shared genes: this was not necessarily so among the enslaved in Jamaica. Here, their given surnames attached the older enslaved to owners rather than to kin, so that people of their race, living in close proximity and sharing names, were just as likely to be work-gang brothers as to be blood brothers. These Africans in Jamaica must have wanted to know, like anyone else, whose blood flowed through their veins. They must have worked out substitute guides to genetic connections. A careful examination of a newly born child to see whether it has the dimples of a particular man must have been one of the ways, and it survives until today in the

African-Jamaican part of the society. The preservation of names dis-carded by the authorities was another. Thus today, Mr John Fyffe of Woodside knows and can share the fact that one of his great-great grand-fathers was Bada Kanali, who was given the name "Hudson", one of those names in the Hopewell list above.[22]

As the preserved name Bada Kanali suggests, the fact and quality of relationship with each other was maintained among the African Jamaicans through such definitive terms as "bada", which translates in English to mean "brother" and which is a term of respectful address to a male relative, usually an elder one, and "tata", very popular in many African languages, which means "father" and is also a term of respect for an elderly person.[23] These forms of address are familiar in the greater Woodside area even today. In such ways the black population in Woodside, St Mary, Jamaica, the New World, maintained their African-ness and kinship ties while participating in a system that bonded them together by owners rather than by blood. Such constructions were part of the mental activity with which those who curried the mules taking the Forbes, the Neilsons, the Burrowes, the Turners and the Pollocks to the review of the militia, who carried their weapons of war, and who worked their sugar and coffee plantations, were engaged.

Enslaved people did not spend all their time in conscious reaction to slavery. Like other workers, many were preoccupied with doing a job well. Thus they took seriously their commissions to get the sugar canes in on time and to make good sugar at the Hopewell estate; to care for the stock in its pen and to keep its butchery a viable business. Coffee production requires less sustained labour than sugar does and the labour-ers have more individual responsibility. These responsible labourers, see-ing to it that the coffee berries were picked on time on the Woodside estate, the Louisiana estate, the Rock Spring, Smailfield, Waterton, Richmond Hill and other coffee estates in the greater Woodside area and other Jamaican and New World estates, were enslaved Africans. It was even possible for these enslaved persons to be sent out on jobs by them-selves. Several white persons depended on the jobbing skills of their enslaved charges to earn them the capital with which eventually to buy themselves an estate. This seems to be the story of Peter McCrae, who in 1817 owned no more reported property than Edward Bryan, Robert Cannon, Richard Christian, Alexander McCrae, Charles McCrae, George McCrae[24] and George Neilson, his slaves, but who, by 1840, with the end of slavery, is now owner of Brae Head, a small property of twenty-five acres.[25]

The traffic in human cargo between Africa and the New World was a serious commercial enterprise intended to provide labour for industries into which large sums of money had been invested. There were several parts to this business and a selection process in each. Selectors in Africa knew that only the best would sell and that only the hardiest could survive a Middle Passage in which captured persons were packaged like sardines, chained and left in their own and their neighbours' faeces for days. Only the physically and mentally fit would reach the auction block in Jamaica. Farquaharson, a possible supplier in St Mary, would choose the best from this auction.[26] So, as the copy of the page of the *Royal Gazette* for 1802 reproduced in figure 3 indicates, slaves for sale were "prime young healthy", were "young healthy and well-disposed", were " coopers by trade".

Physical health, temperament and skill were attributes which the marketers advertised. Some of these skilled persons came from Africa already trained; some were trained in Jamaica. Such persons were sometimes hired out to earn for their masters. Nancy Redwood was one such skilled black woman. She, we can assume from her name, was related to one of Philip Redwood's estates in the nearby parish of St Thomas-in-the-Vale, but between 1832 and 1833 was a part of the workforce of 135 slaves on the Louisiana estate and was hired to J.R. Forbes Esq., of nearby Waterton.[27] She brought in £16 for the estate, which was at this time the property of Peter and Louisa Burnett. Nancy Redwood was one of the skilled black-faced persons in the greater Woodside area, divorced from many human rights but expecting to and making decisions concerning the satisfactory execution of her tasks.

It was not just individuals who jobbed out their charges; estates did so as well. The Woodside estate was one of those which made a considerable amount of money in this way. The jobs reported here were not specialist labour as in the case of Nancy Redwood; this was gang-labour. These African Jamaicans were sent as teams to open up lands at Orange River in 1828 and at Oxford Estate in 1830.[28] In 1828 they laboured at Non-such Estate and on the highways. The evidence of jobbing and of jobbing in gangs points us to another fact: that the enslaved people of Woodside, particularly the men, were involved in going to places outside of the village to work in teams. We can further assume the existence

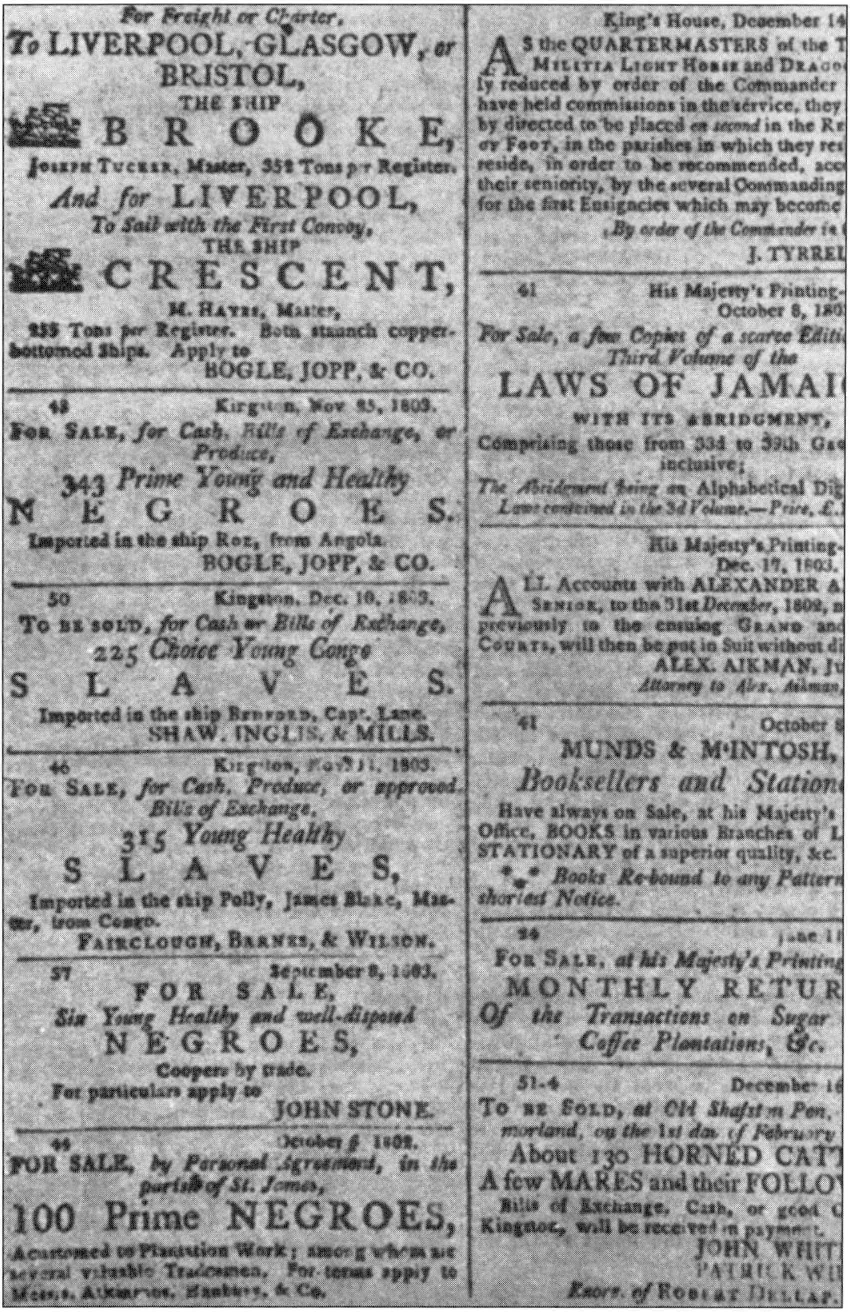

For Freight or Charter,
To LIVERPOOL, GLASGOW, or
BRISTOL,
THE SHIP
BROOKE,
JOSEPH TUCKER, Master, 352 Tons per Register,
And for LIVERPOOL,
To Sail with the First Convoy,
THE SHIP
CRESCENT,
M. HAYES, Master,
235 Tons per Register. Both staunch copper-bottomed Ships. Apply to
BOGLE, JOPP, & CO.

49 Kingston, Nov 25, 1803.
FOR SALE, for Cash, Bills of Exchange, or Produce,
343 Prime Young and Healthy
NEGROES.
Imported in the ship Roe, from Angola.
BOGLE, JOPP, & CO.

50 Kingston, Dec. 10, 1803.
TO BE SOLD, for Cash or Bills of Exchange,
225 Choice Young Congo
SLAVES.
Imported in the ship Bedford, Capt. Lane.
SHAW, INGLIS, & MILLS.

46 Kingston, Nov. 21, 1803.
FOR SALE, for Cash, Produce, or approved Bills of Exchange,
315 Young Healthy
SLAVES,
Imported in the ship Polly, James Blake, Master, from Congo.
FAIRCLOUGH, BARNES, & WILSON.

57 September 8, 1803.
FOR SALE,
Six Young Healthy and well-disposed
NEGROES,
Coopers by trade.
For particulars apply to
JOHN STONE.

44 October 8 1803.
FOR SALE, by Personal Agreement, in the parish of St. James,
100 Prime NEGROES,
Accustomed to Plantation Work; among whom are several valuable Tradesmen. For terms apply to Messrs. Aikman, Hanbury, & Co.

King's House, December 14
AS the QUARTERMASTERS of the T
MILITIA LIGHT HORSE and DRAGO
ly reduced by order of the Commander
have held commissions in the service, they
by directed to be placed en second in the R
of FOOT, in the parishes in which they re
reside, in order to be recommended, acc
their seniority, by the several Commanding
for the first Ensigncies which may become
By order of the Commander in
J. TYRREL

41 His Majesty's Printing-
October 8, 180
For Sale, a few Copies of a scarce Editi
Third Volume of the
LAWS OF JAMAI
WITH ITS ABRIDGMENT,
Comprising those from 33d to 39th Ge
inclusive;
The Abridgment being an Alphabetical Di
Laws contained in the 3d Volume.—Price, £.

His Majesty's Printing-
Dec. 17, 1803.
ALL Accounts with ALEXANDER A
SENIOR, to the 31st December, 1802, n
previously to the ensuing GRAND and
COURTS, will then be put in Suit without di
ALEX. AIKMAN, Ju
Attorney to Alex. Aikman,

41 October 8
MUNDS & M'INTOSH,
Booksellers and Station
Have always on Sale, at his Majesty's
Office, BOOKS in various Branches of L
STATIONARY of a superior quality, &c.
, Books Re-bound to any Pattern
shortest Notice.

34 June 1
FOR SALE, at his Majesty's Printing
MONTHLY RETUR
Of the Transactions on Sugar
Coffee Plantations, &c.

51-4 December 16
To BE SOLD, at Old Shafston Pen,
moreland, on the 1st day of February
About 130 HORNED CAT
A few MARES and their FOLLO
Bills of Exchange, Cash, or good C
Kingston, will be received in payment.
JOHN WHIT
PATRICK WI
Exors. of ROBERT DELLAP.

Figure 3 Detail of a page from the *Royal Gazette*, 17–24 December 1803, taken from *Lady Nugent's Journal of Her Residence in Jamaica from 1801 to 1805*, ed. Philip Wright (Kingston: University of the West Indies Press, 2002), 188.

of a team spirit on such estates, as well as the building of networks with peers outside of greater Woodside.

To feel loyalty and to act accordingly is a human condition. There is at least one report of enslaved workers on one estate in the west of the island teasing those from another about their poor diet and resulting weakness as they push their respective master's loads up a very long and steep hill.

> Slavery time, dem haf fi pull cart from Hampton here to Parade in Montego Bay and pull it up Charlemont hill an come up back and [when dem come to] Bogue dem turn de cart crossways now, and when de oder one dem wan pass, dem ketch quarrel till dem fight. Hampton slave beat dem. Beat de other slave dem. When dem go home, dem master write Mr Taarpe [Tharpe] say mus warn him slave dem not to beat him slave dem again. Mr Taarpe [Tharpe] answer him say mus feed him slave dem and when him feed fi him slave dem, dem will stronger.[29]

This kind of loyalty and camaraderie must have existed too among the Woodside work gangs sent out to labour on the several neighbouring estates. This does not mean that they were totally happy with the absence of human rights that is a part of chattel slavery. In fact the oral accounts tell us that the slaves of the Neilson's estate would ask for time to go to church and spend this time in Daddy Rock, a cave on the estate, planning resistance. That the two states of mind and behaviour would exist together in many of the black folk in greater Woodside is to be expected.

The historian Edward (Kamau) Brathwaite points out that it was the small white settlers who sent their slaves out to work to bring back money to them.[30] The Woodside estate was the largest of the coffee estates in the greater Woodside area but coffee estates were generally perceived in the eighteenth and nineteenth centuries as the small man's business. Dr William John Neilson did job out his slaves and by this token falls in the list of small white settlers. Members of his family fit that definition more closely. With no land of her own, his wife Jane E. Neilson owned in 1832, thirteen slaves.[31] A widow with six children all under twenty-one years of age, Mrs Neilson must have been glad to send her personal enslaved workers out to make money for her. The estate certainly sent some out as carpenters, masons and road labourers to work at Rock Spring and elsewhere in 1836–37.[32] Their labour fetched

£57 8s. 4d., a significant part of the returns of £129 16s. 8d., minus unpriced coffee in stock, for that year. There were other slaves in the greater Woodside area who were the sole property that their masters had, and whose earnings from jobbing would have been a significant source of livelihood for their owners. As shown in the tabulation below (derived from the *Jamaica Almanack*, 1821–1832), Burrowes family members as well as the Pollocks could have operated in this way.

	1821	1824	1826	1832
S.J. Burrowes	12	3	2	–
Frances M. Neilson	8	10	12	15
	1821	1824	1826	1832
J.H. Neilson	6	6	9	–
				(+6 in Dunkeld)
Ann Elizabeth Pollock	1	–	–	–
James Pollock	1	–	–	–
Jane Pollock	2	1	–	–
J.E. Neilson	–	–	–	13

It seems very much from the facts that there were African Jamaicans in the Woodside area who were given to dependent members of white households as capital with which to make a start, much as today's children may be given goats or chickens with which to begin their economic life. Given this economic dependency of white people on the labouring power of their few slaves, there must have been a similar psychological dependency upon them and the motivation to take more care of their health than was then the norm. With her few slaves a significant part of her capital, a proprietor such as Mrs Frances M. Neilson, widowed in 1800, must have been particularly keen to preserve the life, health and the cooperation of the dozen people from whom, in her old age and single life, she made at least a part of her livelihood. There were other people within St Mary and near to the greater Woodside area who were similarly placed – owning slaves and even stock but having no portion of land significant enough to be mentioned in the parish returns.

James Ferguson in 1811 had eighty-seven slaves and four head of cattle.[33] In 1821 another James Ferguson, or perhaps the same person, owned Sterling Castle and seventy-one slaves, while Elizabeth Ferguson, someone in his household, it seems, owned thirteen slaves, and C. Ferguson owned one slave. By 1826 another Ferguson had become a slave owner: Ann now has a slave, but Elizabeth has one fewer.[34] Did Elizabeth give one of her slaves to Ann as a present? John Hermit of Carpenter's Hut in 1821 owned eighteen slaves, one of whom, incidentally, was his namesake.[35] He also owned four head of stock, while P. Hermit of his household owned four slaves. John Hermit continued in 1824 to own the number he did the year before and Patience, no doubt the P. Hermit above, continued to own four slaves. We have met a Patience Hermit as an owner of land;[36] is John her son, and did she hand her property over to him? We cannot say.

The records show that another woman, Elizabeth Timberlake, owned Pleasant Hill Estate, eight slaves and six head of livestock in 1824, but William Timberlake owned just one slave.[37] Was William Elizabeth's son living in her household, as John seems to have been in Patience Hermit's? Hugh D. MacKay owned seven slaves in 1821 and nothing else.[38] He is quite likely the Hugh MacKay who got married at Woodside in that year and who, nine years later, was the overseer there.[39] These owners of such small numbers of slaves, possibly wives or daughters or sons of small landowners, like other small proprietors in Jamaica, would have made their pocket change from hiring out the few African Jamaicans that they owned. Perhaps they restricted their market to others in the area close to or within the greater Woodside area.

These assumptions lead to the further assumption that African Jamaicans were the personal and economic support of the relatively poor white people in the area – wives, children, overseers – who would want to take special care of their miniscule property. We must add that blacks in St Mary also owned slaves, though there is no evidence of this happening in greater Woodside. The Baptist minister of Stewart Town writes in respect of the church and owners of slaves, called apprentices since the Abolition Act of 1834:

> I had forgotten to say that the only member of Stewart Town church who had any apprentices gave them their freedom 1st of August. She is a poor black woman and had nothing else to depend upon. They were *four* in number. Both the churches are now free from that stain.[40]

Close and caring attention would have been given to some blacks in the greater Woodside area, especially those in whose jobbing potential

lay the livelihood of their owners. Such an approach was likely to be
rewarded by kindly sentiments on the part of the enslaved and could
guarantee the return of one sent on a job, such as Miss Nancy Redwood.
It could even be that all slaves were treated kindly. Selina Montague and
Edward Beckford of Woodside certainly were. They were to be manumitted according to the terms of William John Neilson's will, at his death.
He even made plans for their care after manumission: "they were to be
allowed to reside on Woodside Plantation and enjoy the Negro grounds
during their life time".[41] They would have been well treated during his
lifetime and, like Nancy Redwood, were likely to have returned from
any mission on which they were sent.

Length of time together increases sentiment, and sometimes that sentiment is positive. The Edward Beckford above, whose real name had
been Cato, was about four years older than the master, being thirty years
old in 1817 when William John was about twenty-six. Cato had been
part of William John's workforce at least since 1817 and perhaps before,
for he was a creole, born to a mother, Christmas, who was also in the
service of William John. Cato was one of seventy-year-old Christmas's
four sons, aged twenty-eight to forty in 1817. Part of a closely knit and
possibly loving family, Cato could have given comfort, solace and loyalty to a master.

Selina, to be manumitted at his death, according to the terms of
William John's will, was a twenty-year-old sambo girl in 1817, whose
mother was a slave with the Neilson name. Chances are that Selina's
mother was one of William John's father's slaves, and loyal to him.
Selina's sambo twin sisters, aged sixteen in 1817, and who carry the
name of Neilson, were not so fortunate. Nor is there any word on the
possible manumission of Selina's daughters: Queen, one year old in 1817,
and Nadalina Frances Walker, one-and-a-half years old in 1820. Did the
master expect that emancipation would come soon and that they would
in the normal course of time be free? Why then was Margaret Conochie,
the three-year-old daughter of Isabella Bele, a twenty-two-year-old Negro
creole known as Rachel, manumitted in 1820, according to the slave
returns for Woodside proper? Or was her manumission a gift from someone else? If the doctor had given her her freedom, that would be another
mother who would have been grateful to him and another person whose
loyalty he was perhaps rewarding.

J.R. Forbes of Waterton could not count on loyalty from all his enslaved persons. Antonio, aged twenty-two, ran away from him; on 18 April 1826 J.R. had to commit James Forbes to Dr McIntyre's work-house.[42] James, sharing his master's surname, was quite likely with this master in his pre-baptism years or even born as his current master's property. Clearly he and his could-be first master were not getting on well together. Oral reports about the Neilsons that live on today carry a resentment which suggests that though Selina Montague and Edward Beckford might have liked them, not all their other slaves did. Those reports, handed down even to today, portray the Neilson's final heir as a drunkard who sold his patrimony bit by bit to feed his habit; his mother is cast as a proud woman who gets the proverbial fall. And they had their runaways too: their fifty-year-old creole, Thomas Howard, made illegal tracks out of there, as we see from the slave returns for 1817. Nothing in the archival sources indicates that intention equalled actuality and that Selina and Edward were manumitted in deed.

Chapter 5

Woodside and Freedom

Prelude

"An Act for the abolition of Slavery throughout the British Colonies, for promoting the Industry of the manumitted slaves and for compensating the persons hitherto entitled to the service of such slaves . . ." came into being on the first day of August 1834.[1] This act, made and passed in "the 3rd and 4th reign of the present Majesty [William]" aligned the changing of the status of the 311,070 enslaved people in Jamaica with concerns that they be occupied with work and that their former masters be compensated.[2] The latter concern was fairly easily managed. Jamaican slave owners, along with those in the rest of the British colonies, were given £20 million to be divided among them. In effect, the British government, in Biblical language, redeemed the enslaved Jamaican with cash.

Lack of faith that blacks had a philosophy that regarded work positively, and a belief that the continued development of the island required that their labour be available to their ex-owners, tied strings to the gift of freedom. The resulting gift was, in the first place, an apprenticeship to freedom. Ex-slaves, now to be called apprentices, would be required to work for their ex-owners in order to receive their former allowances of food, clothing, medical care and housing. This they were to do for forty-one-and-a-half hours of the week; for the rest, they would practise real freedom, working for whom they wished for wages. Thus was translated the concern for "promoting Industry of the manumitted slaves".

The British government and the Jamaican government which it left to work out the details of "promoting the Industry of the manumitted slaves", did not really see the change mandated by the Abolition Act in terms of a revolution in how both ex-slave and ex-master perceived each other. They very often viewed change in more limited terms – keeping African Jamaicans at work; and not merely at work, but at work in the stations in which the act had found them, only this time round, for pay. Social action was thus defined in economic terms and the presenting need was the conservation of the estates. Thus reform was seen in terms of hours of labour. Little emphasis was placed on social or psychological reform, on the perceptions the formerly enslaved and the former owners had of each other as a prelude to working in a new order.

Tremendous difficulties arose in Jamaica in this area. Freedom of a people lifted out of their country and enslaved, people enslaved here for centuries with little access to social mobility even after they had found a way of redeeming themselves, was freedom of angry people who could have little faith that the society would work for the release of the potential which they knew they had. Freedom required a change in the attitude of the formerly enslaved towards the society. It meant, for him, relating as an independent person with someone who had been accustomed to thinking of and treating him as an owned article. It meant, for the former master, reorienting his perspective to see a black person, even one working for him, as master of his own fate.

In spite of these terms, the ex-slaves were very prayerful and peaceful on 1 August 1834, and went back to work on the following work day. Their defence of rights to their free time against the encroachment of planter interests, however, set off controversies between the Jamaican Assembly and the British government, controversies that resulted in the proclamation of emancipation on 1 August 1838 instead of 1840. By this proclamation the ex-slaves were totally free, and ex-slave and master left to establish what relationships they could.

During the apprenticeship period, a device was introduced into the island to punish wayward labourers in what was thought then to be a more humane and work-oriented fashion. This was the treadmill. That it is reported to have been found in a village close to the greater Woodside area indicates that the planter and ex-slaves here, as elsewhere in the years immediately preceding full freedom, were having disagreements. Interestingly, this oral report comes from Essex where, the archival sources attest, John Grant the overseer was brought before the courts on the petition of P. Davis, an apprentice, and charged twenty shillings for ordering him to be "switched".[3]

An administrative instrument introduced to facilitate social and economic change and which could, it was thought, most closely effect psychological change and social peace, was the stipendiary magistracy. Paid magistrates, mostly retired army officers recruited from Britain, they were, among other things, to handle disputes between ex-masters and ex-slaves. The stipendiary magistrate in charge of Louisiana for the apprenticeship period was T. Watkins-Jones; for Richmond Hill, it was John Harris and for the rest of the greater Woodside area it was R.S. Lambert.[4] After emancipation, the whole parish in which greater Woodside falls, as well as the parishes of Metcalfe and St George, were managed by Alexander Gordon Fyfe/Fyffe, one whom the archival records often refer to by the title, "captain".[5] Fyfe's archival profile looks very much like that of the Captain Alexander Gordon Fyfe, whom Mr John Fyffe of today's Rock Spring claims as his great-grandfather. According to his reputed great-grandson, Captain Fyfe kept the jail at Rock Spring.[6] There are in this area ruins that the community memory calls "station". This, it says, was the jail in slavery days. The Captain Fyfe of the governor's dispatches was indeed inspector of prisons in the 1860s, and as such likely to have had something to do with the jail at Rock Spring.[7]

This could-be Fyffe descendant claims that Captain Fyfe took as his mistress Mother Lindsay, who was also his housekeeper. The birth and baptismal records for the area do mention a family of Lindsays,[8] and the map of 1880 shows a longhouse at Rock Spring marked "Fyffe House" where the Lindsays, according to Mr John Fyffe and other informants, lived. Alexander Gordon Fyfe, well respected by a range of governors, is quite likely to have had residences in more than one parish, given the distances he had to cover.[9] In fact, the official records speak of him as living in St Mary and Portland simultaneously. Alexander Gordon Fyfe's full name has been handed down from generation to generation in Mr John Fyffe's family, and today one of his brothers carries this name. Other archival and oral sources meet in chapter 6 to indicate that this stipendiary magistrate and eventual custos of Portland could have lived in the greater Woodside area, participating at a private as well as a public level in the affairs of the area after 1840.

What were the identities of the people in greater Woodside between whom Harris, Watkins-Jones, Lambert and, later, Captain Fyfe would intervene? We know that Hugh Donald MacKay was still helping with the running of the Woodside plantation; that John Stevens was helping with the running of Waterton; that Thomas of Smailfield had died and that his estate was being run by James Smith, and that Sam Rogers was still running Louisiana.[10] These might have been white, like the Neilson clerks Hugh Mason and Joseph Gray, whom we met in chapter 3. Did any of them have an altercation with their labourers over remuneration and time allocation which needed the stipendiary magistrate's intervention? We know that at Gibraltar Estate in St George, served like most of the greater Woodside area by the same stipendiary magistrate, the overseer attempted to encroach on the apprentices' time, that they refused to work, and that the stipendiary magistrate was summoned to discipline them; that in the aftermath the estate's trash house was set on fire and the workers refused to put it out.[11] Did any of greater Woodside's managers similarly offend any apprentices, creating animosity and the need for the stipendiary magistrate to be called in? We know too that Widow Neilson was still there, and that Waterton, Smailfield, Louisiana and Hopewell were still in business. Waterton and Woodside were, up until 1837, still jobbing out the labour of their apprentices.[12]

Animosity existed, and did flare up in a part of Stipendiary Magistrate Harris's domain.[13] On the Gyles's property in Recess, an administrator kicked a female apprentice in the "belly". With Stipendary Magistrate Watkins-Jones, Harris intervened, taking the woman's complaint to the desk of the Colonial Office. No such distress in the life of the apprentice was reported for the parts of the greater Woodside area which fell under the jurisdiction of these two officers. On the contrary, concerning Richmond Hill, then the property of the McPhersons, Harris reports that the apprentices "have an abundance of provisions; they sell a good deal; their fields are in very good condition".[14] The news for Hopewell is similar. T. Watkins-Jones tells us that the apprentices have lots of provisions and "are offering yams of the best quality for sale at 4/2d [four shillings and tuppence] per cwt".[15] It was the apprentices' approach to serving on the ex-masters' farm that bothered the magistrate. Watkins-Jones complains of the apprentice in St Thomas-in-the-Vale who will say, "Massa me tired; gib me money for me two days; me no work no more, me can't mi good Massa".[16] The speaker, according to Watkins-Jones, will proceed to town "with goods even if he can sell it half way". The apprentices were enjoying their freedom; the master class was not always enjoying their labour as the Emancipation Act had hoped. The apprenticeship period had two years lopped from it.

Stipendiary magistrates helped master and ex-slave to determine the cost of manumission. Lambert might have been summoned by Diana Wilson and Jestina Sewell between 1836 and 1837, to help in determining how much they should pay Mrs Neilson for the un-expired term of their apprenticeship. The sum they each paid to Widow Neilson of Woodside proper was £35.[17] It seems a fair amount: that paid by people in the surrounding areas of Flint River, Essex and Berry Hill was, according to the records, £37.[18] But these sums were not enough to stave off collapse.

External conditions had encouraged plantation owners of greater Woodside to go into coffee production at the end of the eighteenth century and external conditions helped to ruin their coffee businesses. Haiti had been the world's largest producer of coffee but political disturbances there distressed the industry, creating a place in the market for others. Jamaican planters entered the breach.[19] By 1799 there were 686 coffee estates in Jamaica, 27 of which were in St Mary. Woodside, Smailfield, Waterton and Rock Spring were in this number. Less than fifty years after, with Brazil and Ceylon now in the industry, 465 coffee works in Jamaica were abandoned as unprofitable. Six were abandoned in St Mary, four of which were in greater Woodside.[20]

Adding to the problems arising out of competition was the dislocation caused by the emancipation of the enslaved. Sugar estates, like the coffee estates, faced labour problems, and some, Palmetto Grove included, were officially listed as abandoned between 1832 and 1846.[21] Lady Nugent, contemplating Hopewell's beauty in 1802, had questioned the business practices of the Jamaican planter. She had said, "It is wonderful the immense sums of money realized by sugar in this country, and yet all the estates are in debt."[22] For planters who could not keep their estates out of debt, competition and a labour force that, with emancipation, worked with whom and for whom it wished would be crippling blows. How did the estates in the greater Woodside area face these new hurdles?

Some estate owners reacted by selling their estates. Thus Dean sur-
rendered Palmetto Grove to M.J. Purrier and Crossman sold Smailfield
to Richard Thomas.[23] Some sold only a part of the estate: it appears that
the Burrowes family kept only twenty of their Rock Spring acres and
sold one hundred to Dr Alexander Cooke,[24] who would later become
the member of the House of Assembly for St Mary.[25] Peterswold of
Petersfield made similarly drastic changes. By 1836 he had handed over
that part of Petersfield called Cottage to members of his family.[26] In 1839
Thomas, the new owner of Smailfield, was conveying it to five people
in equal shares – David Morris, Robert Thomas, Robert Hinds, George
Ludlow and Mary Burrowes.[27] Were these children and in-laws?

The first clear evidence of sale of Woodside proper is that which
took place in 1842. In that year Jane Eliza, executrix of William John
Neilson's estate, and George William Neilson, his heir, now apparently
twenty-one years old or over, officially parted with six acres and one
rood in the middle of their holding. This they sold to William Cousins
for £31 5s. William Cousins is likely to be "Sandy alias William Cosens",
who had been among the enslaved of Dr Neilson in 1817 if not before.
William was a creole, twenty-six years old then, and the son of a woman,
Lucy alias Lizzy Williams, who was then fifty-five years old, born in
Africa and, like her son, part of Dr Neilson's property. The transfer
document was witnessed by Gilbert McNab on 23 November 1842.[28]
McNab was at the time the doctor in charge of the jail. There was one
such institution at Rock Spring and McNab must have been a frequent
visitor in the area. Cousins's land was surrounded by Neilson land. He
and it remained a part of the family, clearly!

From the days of Father John, the Neilsons had had property beyond
Louisiana, in what seems like today's Pear Tree Grove.[29] It is possible
that this property in the parish of St Catherine, then called St Thomas-
in-the-Vale, had been sold to become the Woodside mentioned in the
1829 and 1832 returns as owned by John Ewart.[30] It is quite likely too
that they had had more than the 734 acres in St Mary that we see them
with in 1840, and that this excess was sold to the Burnetts of Louisiana,
whom we see in 1840 owning 181 acres in St Mary along with their St
Thomas-in-the-Vale holding.[31] Palmetto Grove's time, according to the
available records, came in 1842 when it sold four acres.[32] From thence
we find a division of that property into very small holdings, sometimes
as small as an acre. By 1846 that part of the estate that was nearest to

Home Castle was sold out in one- and two-acre plots, and arrangements were being made to sell another set, this time of three-acre lots.[33] Windsor Castle, as we have already mentioned, was a small settlers' colony by 1843. Hopewell stood firm until later in the century.[34] How about the people who had laboured on these estates?

Black reaction to freedom no doubt took the forms in Woodside that it took in other parts of Jamaica. Some formerly enslaved persons bolted, according to oral reports, from Orange Hill about fourteen miles away and ran to a place still called Over-the-River, worried that Pharoah's army would follow them,[35] and hoping that, as for the children of Israel, a body of water could be used by Jehovah to hold back the advancing enemy horde. There, near the banks of the river, they established a community still called Jubilee. And we know of course of the several free villages established with the help of missionaries. There is no evidence of any such activity in the Woodside area; nevertheless it is more than likely that there were conglomerations of freed people living together here in emotional bonds.

Some historians claim that estate owners were very aware that a lonely slave was an unhappy one and an unhappy one, a difficult one. They therefore tried not to sell or buy individuals unless they were domestics or tradesmen.[36] William John Neilson must have been thinking along these lines when he bought the hundred-acre plot which looks like today's John Crow Hill–Jumper area, for he bought the lands with the slaves on it.[37] Under these circumstances, people in this sub-area of Woodside would be well known to each other and would have built up their own ways of dealing with each other. Oral reports support this theory: Arnold Remikie/Ramiki advised that the John Crow Hill–Jumper just mentioned came into the twentieth century with a population bound together in religious practices found nowhere else in the greater Woodside area.[38] We note too that it was common for enslaved persons to be sent out to work on other estates in gangs. Given this fact, members of field gangs were likely to have known each other well and to have established bonds between themselves which went beyond the masters' definition of their purpose.

After emancipation, there was still work to be done on estates and for the parish authorities. It is quite conceivable that, as is written for other parts of Jamaica, freed persons in the greater Woodside area bonded emotionally in gangs, continued to go from estate to estate seeking and doing work in teams, thus reinforcing their sense of community. The freedmen were human: several, instead of continuing to work in the old haunts in their communities, or out of it in gangs, would have left the area or shifted between the area and elsewhere in search of friends and relatives who had been separated from them for whatever reason. There would also be those highly individualized persons prepared to work for themselves at whatever cost; and there must have been those who chose to see the fact of freedom as the right to laze about.

During slavery, there had been laws specifying how the enslaved ought to be treated.[39] One such law stipulated that jackets and petticoats were to be supplied to females once per year, and jackets and drawers to men once per year; and that an acre of land was to be made available for every five slaves, for them to supply themselves with food. Another act required that masters give the enslaved one day in every fortnight, and every Sunday, except in the crop season, for them to conduct their own affairs. These two requirements contributed to the development of a vibrant small-farming industry and internal marketing system. It seems logical that this would be even more so in the coffee-growing areas such as greater Woodside. Work in coffee did not require the total involvement that sugar's crop time demanded. Given this circumstance, the enslaved worker here would have had more opportunity to develop a work plan relative to his own cultivation and more time at his disposal to see to the actualization of this programme.

Woodside Estate and Waterton Estate, and no doubt others in the area, had indeed jobbed out their labourers, taking them outside of the reach of their provision grounds. The requests for labour from outside agencies seem, however, to have been intermittent, leaving the enslaved of the Woodside area with sufficient time in which to plan and carry out their projects towards establishing themselves as farmers. We can expect that Woodside's slaves would have been part of the traffic to the markets to sell their ground provisions and buy whatever suited their tastes.

It was illegal for the enslaved to own property. Legally, whatever they had belonged to their masters. It was not until 1826, twelve years before emancipation, that they were given by law the right to own property. Still, this right had certain qualifications, for ownership of anything that was valued at more than £20 could be contested by their master in the Supreme Court. It was customary for masters to waive their right over what the enslaved produced in their spare time. Firearms and horses were items that they strongly felt should not be in the hands of the enslaved. We can see, from the above, that the enslaved people of greater Woodside are likely to have been accustomed to the use of money, to trading and marketing, and to have been in a position to supplement the wardrobe of annual drawers and jackets and petticoats given them by their masters. These master-given ones would have been their "drudging" clothes; they could afford to buy clothes for special occasions. Freedom would have found them with a small-farming and a trading mindset, a sense of time management, a notion of economic action on the basis of a thought-out plan, some money, some material goods, and even livestock to trade in the animal market four miles away, between Dean Pen and Highgate, which oral reports intimate existed at the time. These activities would have created and fostered a sense of group and community solidarity.

Those of the enslaved who were so minded would have turned their energies to religion. The lists of those baptized into the Anglican faith between 1817, the year of the compulsory registration of slaves, and 1834, the date of the promulgation of the Abolition Act, is long. Were they forced to baptize their children, or was baptism by their own determination? Whatever the situation, Reverend Archer, one of the official island curates, resided in that part of greater Woodside called Rock Spring, until his death in 1841, and would have been seen daily as he went about his business on horseback; he would have been well within reach of those who needed his religious guidance.[40] He might have had to suggest Christian names. One was no longer just Othello, Scotland or Christmas;[41] one had two English names and sometimes three, as we have seen from the list of slaves in the preceding chapter. On what occasions would the clothes that they had bought themselves be used? Certainly to enter the Anglican church for baptism and other festive occasions; for the Christmas party, which was likely to be supported financially by the master, as was the custom in Jamaica. Then there were Sundays, which belonged to the enslaved: on this day they could dress in their finery and go off to the market, whether as vendor or as buyer.

On the estate for which we have this kind of information, Woodside, there were fifty-four African-born people in 1817, as we see in the slave returns.[42] Among these were five women aged sixty to eighty. That three creoles were named Quaco, Quamin and Cuffee indicates that Africa was not forgotten. It is hardly likely that the African religions would be forgotten either. A Ghanaian tale and West African styles of cooking remain here today; why not religious practices? The *manalva* – thought to be a corruption of the Ghanaian "Nana Rebo", meaning the "Queen is coming" – may be the remnant of the annual odwira festival.[43] In this Woodside rite, there is one queen dressed in finery, there are courtiers to protect her and there are soldiers who want to seize her. A whole night, with many changes of the queen's garments, is spent in the protecting of this majesty, and in her dancing her way out of the reach of the would-be snatchers to the sound of drumbeat and songs with the word-sounds of Africa.[44]

On Woodside Estate there was, in 1817, one American slave. He was Jacob "alias John Neilson"; he was forty years old. On the neighbouring Palmetto Grove Estate, there were at that time forty-four American-born slaves, all over forty years old and many carrying the surname of their old slave-master, Wright.[45] On the Goshen estate, about fourteen miles away, was Gibb, an itinerant enslaved preacher born in America, who was known to function in St Mary and St Thomas-in-the-Vale.[46] The greater Woodside area stretched across these parishes. It stands to reason that the proselytizing Gibb, given the existence of people of his nationality in greater Woodside, would have found his way here.

Barry Chevannes tells us that another black American Baptist preacher had been invited by a Quaker planter to Christianize his slaves.[47] Could the proselytizing of the enslaved through the medium of American enslaved and free Baptist preachers have been a policy among Quakers in Jamaica? Mary Gibb, who is likely to have been Gibb's mistress, averred in 1820 that she was a Quaker.[48] Under the slave lists of several planters in the greater Woodside area in 1820 we see "if a Quaker, affirm" preceding their signatures. It was so for Dr Neilson of Woodside, for Peterswold of Petersfield, and for Clark and Pollock of the Stapleton area, for instance. It could be that they were Quakers before 1820 and that they, like Mary Gibb, must have supported and even invited the black American Baptist to missionize their enslaved workers – Peterswold in particular: where others used the word "alias" to distinguish Christian names from other names, he created categories in his returns, captioned "old name" and "christian name".[49]

Gibb practised a kind of Baptist religion in which candidates being prepared for baptism were encouraged to spend nights in the wilderness praying and waiting for the spirit. This kind of religion, in which the spirits, nature and the Christian God are so entwined, is called Myal. It is a mix between Christianity and African religions and prizes natural formations such as unusual caves and rocks. These were and are aplenty in the greater Woodside area. In fact, the American anthropologist Martha Beckwith mentions the existence in Jamaica of an Africa-derived deity called Long Bubby Susan, and on the Woodside plantation there was and is a rock carving officially recognized as Arawak/Taino that was called by this name and which Mrs Vie Campbell, one of the Hermits/Hermitts who grew up here, says was associated with African word-sounds.[50] The accounts of other old people tell us that the enslaved people met in another cave, Daddy Rock, to discuss their own business.[51]

The elements for the establishment of the Gibb form of Baptist practice, Myalism, were all here – black American slaves, natural geological formations and African religious retentions. There are signs in existing cults that this mix was here. The signs exist in the oral tradition, and have been written about by Beckwith. There is still word here of the water maid, the bongo men able to perform superhuman feats, and we read of the wonders of Fifee Bogle, the Myal man from Woodside.[52] It is commonly thought by historians and anthropologists that Myal and the more orthodox British Baptist practice co-existed in one unit. It is likely that they did so in Woodside as elsewhere.[53]

African rites were frowned on by the establishment and had to be practised in secret; hardly an occasion for showing off one's finery. The orthodox English Baptists, by February of 1831, were offering greater Woodside's enslaved a legitimate occasion for dress. Meetings in their new church, like the Anglican services but unlike Myal ceremonies, would have required the wearing of European clothes on some occasions, with the consequent expense. This English Baptist church was flourishing here, indeed, shortly before emancipation.

> On the 2d of this month, [February] I baptised 15 persons and commenced a church at Bray [Brae] Head, a place in the mountains, about eleven miles from Port Maria . . . . The church at Bray Head, of the formation of which I gave you an account in my last, goes well. There are now several candidates for baptism, and the people are building themselves a place to meet in, the one we have being much too small. It is very pleasing to see what numbers flock to hear the word of life, even on week-day evenings, though most of them have to labour in the fields until dark.[54]

Thus wrote the English Baptist minister Reverend Bayliss, who was stationed at the mother church in Port Maria.

Going to this church was not a totally happy affair. By 1831, when the Baptists set up their church in greater Woodside, the whites in Jamaica, already socially, militarily and legally organized as a superior tribe, were beginning to fear the spectre of organized blacks which arose with the establishment of churches outside of the state-sanctioned one. The House of Assembly had proposed the Consolidated Slave Act in 1826, by which enslaved people found guilty of preaching and teaching "as anabaptists or otherwise" without permission from their owners and the quarter sessions of the parish, would be punished by whipping, or imprisonment in the workhouse at hard labour.[55] In addition, the proposal stated, no "sectarian minister, or other teacher of religion" would be allowed to keep his place of meeting open between sunset and sunrise, and any religious teacher taking money from slaves would be fined £20 and sentenced to a month in jail if he did not pay this fine.

The proposal was rejected by the British government, but that it passed the Jamaican House is evidence of the local whites' fear of organizations of blacks over which they had no control. In the year that the English Baptists were so busily setting up the Brae/Bray Head church, Sam Sharpe, an enslaved person and a English Baptist deacon with Myal connections, organized a strike of labourers in the west of the island which turned into the uprising that those whites who framed the Consolidated Slave Act had feared. We can well imagine the talk and the "I-told-you-sos" that faced McCrae, Peterswold or whoever it was that had given permission for the Baptists to meet on his property.

By 1832 a Colonial Church Union had been formed for the express purpose of destroying non-Anglican churches, not just by the spiritual tactics but by concrete aggression — the burning of churches. The Port Maria Baptist church was burned down in 1835.[56] We have no evidence to prove a connection with the Colonial Church Union, but he who did it – unnamed in the records – rode out and hanged himself. Blacks did not own horses. Port Maria was Brae/Bray Head's mother church and naturally suffered with it. The oral reports state that the Brae/Bray Head church was subsequently taken over by the Anglicans,[57] who, the records tell us, were pastored by Reverend Girod and Reverend Archer, whom they also show had been doing a great many baptisms and some marriages of slaves in the area at that time.[58] There is no record of when the church was actually taken over by the Anglicans.

Between 1817 and 1834, 390 enslaved persons were baptized into the Anglican faith. This was about one third of the enslaved people in the greater Woodside area. Only one or two of those registered in 1817 and 1820 as slaves on Dr Neilson's estate were listed among these 390. Several slaves on that estate had been baptized, as we see from the fact that they have two names in Woodside proper's slave returns. These must have been baptized into the English Baptist faith and remained there, or retreated into the more African Baptist/Myal. The same can be said for other estates. Between 1818 and 1831 Palmetto Grove and its pen had sometimes as many as 327 enslaved persons. Only forty-two of them became Anglicans at this time, although nearly all of its predominantly American and African population have two English names. It seems to have been the younger slaves on the Woodside estates who turned to Anglicanism.

Whatever the situation, as a result of the religious activity of the Anglicans some of the enslaved converted their unions to marriage in accordance with Christian orthodoxy, European style. These conversions were relatively few and obviously the result of some meditation on the part of the couple, who must have been thinking of more than the travails of enslavement. These marrying couples in all cases lived on the same estate and in some cases bore the same last names. These surnames are not always those of their current masters, indicating that these enslaved had a history that preceded their present estate history. There is evidence of marriages in 1830 between the enslaved persons Henrietta Morrison and Thomas Downs of Woodside, between Simon Taylor and Mary Brice of Hopewell, and between John Forrester and Amelia Mitchell of Petersfield. Amelia was one of those baptized between 1817 and 1831.

Thomas Downs is likely to have been the "England alias Thomas Downs" of Dr Neilson's slave returns for 1817, reproduced above with an asterisk against his name, as I have done for all the key enslaved people mentioned in this work. The Thomas Downs mentioned in the 1817 returns was a Negro creole, twenty-eight years of age. He was the son of Nancy, then a fifty-year-old African who had given to the Woodside estate other sons – Cuffee, alias Alick Donaldson, two years Thomas's junior; Jupiter, alias George Wellington, two years Thomas's senior; and Othello, who was ten years younger than Thomas. There were other Downses on the estate. There was Charlotte, born in Africa, unlike her other namesakes. Charlotte was thirty years old in 1817, and by then had produced for the estate the one-year-old Quaco, alias Tom Downs. She had also given the estate Louisa, alias Letitia Russell, aged six in 1817, and Prudence, one year old in 1820. Was this lady, registered in the returns as Quiano (writing unclear) alias Charlotte Downs, the sister of Thomas? No mother's name is listed for Charlotte: they were probably only related by virtue of having served the same master, Downs, before their arrival at the Woodside estate.

Henrietta Morrison, Thomas Downs's wife, had also been among Dr Neilson's enslaved workers in 1817, as we see from the slave returns reproduced here. She had been listed as a Negro creole who had been called "Cathery" (writing not clear). She was fourteen years old in 1817, fourteen years younger than Thomas. She was the child of Belinda, alias Fidelia Morrison, who was, in 1817, a thirty-five-year-old African-born slave who was the property of Dr Neilson and who also gave the Woodside estate Princess Love Morrison, aged three years old in 1817. Other Woodside Morrisons are also joined. In 1818 Lydia Morrison and Angus Morrison consecrate their union. Are they related by kin or by service to a common master prior to joining Dr Neilson's workforce? No Lydia Morrison is on the estate's returns for the years 1817 to 1832, but there is a Lydia alias Rosanna Beckford who would be a teenager at this time. Was this the Lydia who marries Angus? Are Lydia and Angus related to Henrietta? Angus, who had been Billy before he assumed his alias, was a forty-year-old Jamaican-born creole in 1817, at least twenty years older than Lydia of Dr Neilson's workforce. Angus's mother's name is not listed in the records.

In April of the year that Lydia Morrison and Angus Morrison of Woodside were joined, Edward Brien and Janet Walker of Petersfield were also joined; on 19 July William Thomas and Louisa Grant, and William Fraser and Elizabeth Watt, both couples from Hopewell, were married. In December it was the time of George Mitchell and Eleanor Peters of Petersfield, and on Christmas Day Edward Williams and Sarah Glenny of Woodside celebrated their marriage. In 1832 the marriage of Daniel Coutrice and Kezie Campbell of Hopewell was solemnized, and in 1834, when the status "slave" gave way to "apprentice", Charles Grant and Juliana Grant solemnized theirs, Reverend Archer from Rock Spring officiating. That each marrying couple lived on the same estate suggests that they might have been already in unions, spending their mental energy on thinking about the betterment of themselves and their families, and on the issue of enslavement only when it forced itself upon them.

Ancestors-to-Be

With the legal end to slavery, African Jamaicans, at least as far as baptismal recording was concerned, now had fathers. The father's name, along with that of the mother of the child, was now entered into the relevant government records. Surnames now tell of a connection with the father. Subsequent generations of people living in greater Woodside have now to trace their history back to their fathers. Those enslaved men on the various estates in the area have officially become ancestors!

If we look at the list of the approximately 390 names available to us for the estates of greater Woodside, and look at those occurring most frequently, we find the Harrisons as the dominant ancestor in Change Hill. For Hopewell, it is the Browns, Grants, Campbells, Douglases, Greens, Gordons, Hamiltons, Harrises and Hudsons. Louisiana ancestors would be the Burnets/Burnetts, the Stanburys and the Stewarts. There were a variety of names in Palmetto Grove but only one appears more than once: Richards; this is the Palmetto Grove ancestor for the purposes of this work. For Petersfield, it is the Burnetts, McDonalds, Whites, Williamses and possibly the Hibberts. For Richmond Hill, the Hamiltons and Johnstons; for Rock Spring, the Walkers; and for Woodside proper the Conies, Hamiltons, Henrys, Hermits, Neilsons, Richardses, Smiths and Walkers. There were only three enslaved males on the list for Stapleton. We present all three as ancestors: Buchanan, Duncan and Timberlake. Did these men create families that challenged the incumbents in Hopewell Estate and Pen, take over the failing Palmetto Grove sugar estate, the Petersfield–Change Hill Pen, and the dying coffee estates of Woodside proper, Stapleton, Rock Spring, Smailfield, Louisiana and Richmond Hill?

Word on the people named above in the 1840s to 1860s relates to births and deaths and marriages; the data comes from the Island Records Office. Note, however, that only the Anglican births and deaths are listed in the government records and that marriages by other denominations are only listed after 1840. From this source, with its limitations, we note that the Browns, Douglases, Gordons, Hamiltons and Hudsons of Hopewell lost people who bore their surnames and could have been loved ones. In Woodside, a Neilson – Frances – produced a child by Alexander Sheriffe. He bore his father's names, Christian and surname. They were married on Boxing Day 1842. Frances, obviously named after old Mrs Frances Neilson, was born in 1820 to one of the sambo twins surnamed Neilson who were then the property of Dr Neilson. At marriage, Frances was a labourer, as was her husband, who hailed from Lucky Valley. Interestingly this Lucky Valley was in the returns for 1832, listed in the *Jamaica Almanack* along with "Woodside" as owned by the same person. These two properties were in the neighbouring parish of St Thomas-in-the-Vale and owned by John Ewart. We have suggested elsewhere that this "Woodside" could be the part of the Neilson's property that was in or near to Pear Tree Grove, an area which joins St Mary to St Thomas-in-the-Vale. Sheriffe could have come to his master's Woodside in St Thomas-in-the-Vale, espied the beauteous Frances as she laboured on her mistress's Woodside in St Mary, and watched her for four years until marriage was possible. The evidence from oral and archival sources indicates that this couple lived in that part of greater Woodside which is in St Catherine, then called St Thomas-in-the-Vale, and that they left children and grandchildren to carry on the name there.[59]

Over in Stapleton, Mitchell Timberlake, who had been baptized in 1825, twenty years later, in the month of October, gets a son, Mitchell Grant, by Margaret Gordon. During this period some less popular slave names appear as parents in the greater Woodside area. In Palmetto Grove, for instance, though we see no birth, deaths or marriages registered for the Richards whom we had selected as an ancestor, we do find that a Johnstone and a Williams bore children baptized into the Anglican faith. These two names were in the baptismal list for 1818–31 but not with the frequency of Richards. In Change Hill, a Crossman baptized in 1817 or 1818 baptized her child in 1840–60. That there is no mention of the Richards family in these later records could be due to the skew towards the preservation of records of the Church of England: later Richardses could have been baptized in other faiths.

Some names that did not appear in the biased baptismal list of 1817–34 are here in the 1840s and 1850s on the baptismal list. Among these new people are the Hinds of Change Hill. Joseph and Mary Hinds were married and produced a child in 1844. There were others. In that same year, Duncan Richfield and Rosetta Symmonds of Louisiana – new names – produced a child, and in 1845 so did Prince William and Catherine Walker of Palmetto Grove, Robert Green and Mary Bennet of Smailfield, Thomas Campbell and Henrietta Edwards, John Stephens and Sarah Nasmyth, and James Sharp and Sarah Lynch of Woodside.

In Louisiana in 1845, John Mounser and Letitia Thomas and William Brown and Jennie Edwards baptized their children into the Anglican communion, as did their fellow villagers James Watt and Roseyann Bell. In Petersfield, Edward McCaw and Elizabeth McDermott did the same, as did Louis Grant and Gracey Ann Thomas of Waterton. In 1847 Edward and Catherine Cox of Petersfield baptized what was to be one of several children. In 1848 in Stapleton, Jane McBean christened her child; so did William and Clarissa Dixon of Hopewell, and Thomas Latouche and Marina Williams of Palmetto Grove. William and Harriet Hind of Petersfield brought their child into the Anglican communion in the same year. Joseph Hutton and Diana Thompson of Stapleton, Robert Campbell and Jane Shand of Petersfield, and Edward and Anne Edwards did likewise in 1849. Baptism is the beginning of membership in the Anglican Church. The above might not clearly speak of new people entering the greater Woodside area but it does speak, authoritatively, of the growing popularity and potential expansion of the Anglican Church in greater Woodside ten years after emancipation.

Land ownership in the area also increased. Land, of course, does not grow, so increase necessarily means reduction of sizes of pre-existing farms. In 1846 that part of Palmetto Grove near to Home Castle saw David Brice, William Clark, Fred Simpson, William Wright, Oxford Thor/Thaw and Richard Taylor owning one- and two-acre plots.[60] Five of these six surnames appear in the baptismal lists. Thaw was the surname of the owner of Change Hill in 1824; Oxford Thor/Thaw (writing was illegible) is likely to have been his slave. It is fair to say that at least the people mentioned above remained in the area, converting their status from slave to freeholder. Lots of about three acres were surveyed to be sold to George James, Dennis Lord, Nicholas Stevenson, David Shaw, James Graham, a Roberts, Duncan Campbell, George Roberts, James Heslop and David Cruickshank. The last was to get two lots. Only three of these names – the two Roberts and Shaw – are surnames not on the slave baptismal list. These were either not baptized Anglicans or new to the area.[61]

A part of Windsor Castle had by 1840–60 become a virtual township of small proprietors. Their settlement covered 252 acres, one rood and fifteen perches, and ranged from one acre to seven acres per person. The names of the new proprietors are below.[62] Asterisks are beside those not found in the Anglican list of its baptized in greater Woodside, an admittedly incomplete source for identifying the population of enslaved persons in the area. As we can see from the list of new landowners, many surnames had appeared in the baptismal slave list for estates in the greater Woodside area. It is conceivable that ex-slaves and/or their relatives went from the several estates into nearby Windsor Castle to get themselves their own piece of ground. The names of the new Windsor Castle owners are below.

James Grant	Robert Morgan	Joiner(?) Hamilton
Charles Lindsay	George Grant	John Webley*
Joseph Harrison	James Davis	Samuel Sinclair
Charles Roberts	Sarah Forbes	George MacKay*
Billy Ready*	Francis Allen	William McDonald
Richard Henry	Edward Conridge*	Richard Allen
James Crossman	Joe Allen	John Stanbury
Robert Mason Carter*	Richard Thompson	Samuel Sinclair
Robert Thompson	Richard Hines	Huie Dunn*
Carolyn Morgan	Richard Whiteman*	Philip Crossman
William Porteous	Thomas Neilson	John Keys*
Richard Wilson	Rebecca Darling*	Charles Gilbert*
John Bennett	Ralph McClure*	Philip Redwood
Robert Dixon*	Henry Williams	James Thomas
Richard Knight/Wright?	Rodney Harrison	James Carno*

Notice that some surnames are repeated. Siblings or persons who had served the same master might have chosen to seek lands in the same settlement.

There is no obvious gender bias in the lists of the enslaved baptized into the Anglican communion, females being 188 of the 390 listed. The same cannot be said for land ownership, as only three of those listed above are women and their portions are small, falling between three and two acres. The gender bias is apparent in the Palmetto Grove lands sold out in 1846 as well. The land in greater Woodside was being broken up by 1880 into small subdivisions here and there, and being bought by people who could have been slaves on these estates. These people were mostly men, as we see.

Meanwhile, the once popular names disappeared from the Vestry, the militia and the civil list after 1840. Donald MacKay as judge for St Thomas-in-the-Vale, William Parker as clerk of the peace and William Lord as clerk of the Vestry are the only familiar names. The names Lord and Parker are also associated with the militia, the former being a colonel and the latter, a captain. The name Grant also appears in the militia. Where are all the others – the Neilsons, the Forbes, the Turners, the Burrowes, the Burnetts? James H. Neilson, whose wedding in 1821 at Carron Hall Dr William John Neilson had attended,[63] followed him to the grave in 1832.[64] George Paplay/Pupley, no doubt a relative of the Frances Charlotte Paplay/Pupley whom Hugh Donald MacKay wed at Woodside in 1821,[65] went in that year too.[66]

John Rose Forbes of Waterton, now coroner, died in June of 1835.[67] The ceremony was performed not by a priest but by Hugh D. MacKay, by now a magistrate. Reverend James Walter Archer, island curate, was alive and well and living in Rock Spring nearby. Why did he not perform the final rites? Was Forbes not an Anglican, not a Christian? The reverend himself passes on in 1841.[68] Two years later May Turner, possibly of the Smailfield Turners, went,[69] and in 1844[70] Walter Pollock and Alexander Pope, the latter possibly the husband of Maria Jane, who had owned three St Mary estates including Smailfield[71] in 1832.[72] Elizabeth Timberlake of the Stapleton area goes in 1846.[73] There is no word of the death of Jane Eliza Neilson. We know that she and her son George were alive in 1842 and selling part of the Woodside property. Why was it that a newcomer witnessed this land transfer? Why McNab? Where were her old neighbours – the Harrisons, the Harts, the Parkers, the MacKays – with whom the family had done business in days of old?

The old order was changing. True, the Grants and Parkers had had their squabble over land but, this apart, greater Woodside had seemed a closely knit and stable area, in which the major players were relatively large agro-business men and women sending their produce to England and to areas within Jamaica, by sea and land transportation, keeping detailed records of their transactions. They had a retinue of workers of several grades in their businesses. Apart from overseers and slaves, for instance, two Neilson men, one of them James Henry, had clerks, both of whom – Hugh Mason and Joseph Gray – were white and died in 1821.[74] There were among the old owners of Woodside, their own doctor, lawyers, financiers and surveyors. Together they went off to Vestry meetings to decide the fate of the parish, off to barracks to practise to defend the realm and their part of it. Their holdings were kingdoms in which they ruled their large numbers of slaves. There was little variation in the layout of these kingdoms: there was the great house with its name, the coffee or cane fields relatively near to the great house with the slave houses and the works close by, and further away the slave provision grounds. Each unit had its stream nearby. By 1840 this fabric is showing signs of wear and tear as bits of estate lands are wrested out of the hands of the former owners and fissioned into tiny farms. The anthill was opened and the blacks were slowly crawling out.

The old order passed away to the accompaniment of ill will at the national level. The old guard declared war upon its ex-slaves. William Knibb is quoted in the *Baptist Missionary Herald* of June 1845 as saying at a public meeting in England, of the situation in Jamaica:

> to show the animus of these men – as soon as the freeholds had been purchased, there was a demand for white pine, and lumber shingle. The tax was taken off or nearly so, from white and red staves . . . used to make puncheons and hogsheads . . . and the duty on white pine and pitch pine [was increased].[75]

Puncheons, hogsheads and hoops were articles used in the sugar factories owned by the ex-masters. According to this report made in 1845, the pre-emancipation duty on staves used to make the puncheons and hogsheads was twelve shillings; this was reduced to two shillings. The tax on wooden hoops had been four shillings; it was now reduced to one shilling. In contrast, the duty on white pine and pitch pine had been four shillings. Now that the newly emancipated people had bought their bits of land and were ready to put houses on them, using white and pitch pine, the duty was moved to eight shillings for one and twelve shillings for the other.

A great deal of this animus was played out between the nonconformist clergy and the State. A note in the October 1840 issue of the *Baptist Missionary Herald* comments on the New Marriage Act, by which dissenting clergy were now required to charge for performing marriages.[76] Offenders were to be sentenced to twelve months in prison. Marriages were now to cost a dollar and marriages performed before this act had to be back-registered if they were to be valid. According to an article of March 1841 in the same journal, the Anglican Church now had twenty-one incumbents and twenty-one curates receiving £500 and £400 per annum each, plus "glebe", as the lands available for the clergyman's personal use were called. It had a total of seventy-six ministers of all grades, most paid from the government coffers, so that "annual income derived by the clergy from parish taxes, the island chest, the glebe lands and slave compensation money including salaries paid to bishops and archbishops amounts to £40,000 and the House of Assembly proposed to double the number of island curates".[77]

The Anglican clergy was obviously seen by the powers that be as a means of keeping the fraying fabric together, of putting the ants back in the anthill or controlling their upward mobility. Taxing house-building material reduced the quantum of cash available for buying land. This was obviously another way of halting the fragmentation of the plantations. The coalitions were now the State and the Anglicans versus the newly freed and the nonconformist clergy. It was the feeling that such a cleavage existed that prompted Reverend Day of the Baptist church in Port Maria to declare in the *Baptist Missionary Herald* of 1841 that some ministers were applying to the House of Assembly for grants to assist them in building their churches but that he preferred to preach in the open air rather than beg them for help.[78] This Reverend Day, according to Swithin Wilmot, was instrumental in bringing ex-slaves together in St Mary to defeat a white proprietor in the election for the House of Assembly.[79] One issue which Reverend Day used to galvanize support was the issue of immigration. Only one black person, however, voted in this 1844 election in the greater Woodside area – he was a Williams, a shopkeeper – but every vote counted.[80]

Feeble though their voting power was, the people of the area would be aware of and take to heart the sentiments, fissures and new coalitions which had come with their emancipation. They were aware, for instance, of the proposal to break up the parish of St Mary and to make the eastern part of it, with part of St George, into the parish of Metcalfe. Alexander Gordon Fyfe, who at the time managed an estate near to Annotto Bay and who lived in St Mary, quite likely Rock Spring, as well as in St George, favoured the change, and in 1843 he was made stipendiary magistrate of this new parish.[81] He continued to be stipendiary magistrate of St Mary and St George. According to this official, giving evidence before a committee in 1842, Reverend Archer, the Anglican cleric, who as we know lived in Rock Spring and worked in the area, held a contrary position and had got "some peasants" to petition against it. The peasants' fear, Fyfe opined, was that their pastor, the same Reverend Archer, would be taken away from them. Clearly, whatever had been the intention of the political authorities in introducing Anglican curates into the lives of the enslaved and freed slaves, bonding with them did take place, bringing them together into a political position and political action.

By the time the issue of the breaking up of St Mary came to a solution, Reverend Archer had passed away. It could have been his influence, however, which made it possible for Fyfe to say in his testimony concerning the reverend's former clients: "while they maintain their own rights, they are ready to acknowledge the rights of others", a statement which those who had designed the reconstruction of the society ought to have been happy to hear. Woodside's new people had, despite their history, a democratic streak.

Chapter 6

The New Woodside People

Families continued to grow in the greater Woodside area from the 1850s onwards, according to the relevant official figures. Some of these names that we are now meeting as baptized Anglicans, are not surnames we met on the list of baptized Anglican slaves.[1] In Woodside in 1850, Thomas and Ruth Francis produced a child; two years later Charles McClure and Isabella Abrahams produced, as did George and Sarah Prince, and in 1856, Henry and Selma Conneridge. John Elisha Walker was born and baptized in that year too; the records do not say who his parents were. In Smailfield we meet the family who might have produced Mother Lindsay,[2] the housekeeper and the mother of the child of Stipendiary Magistrate Fyfe. In 1837 Robert and Jane Lindsay had produced a female child. Was this child the younger sister of the woman who was to become Fyfe's concubine, Mother Lindsay? Was Mother Lindsay Robert's sister, the aunt of this child of Jane and Robert?

Another Smailfield couple who bore fruit which was duly baptized in the Anglican faith in the 1850s, was Henry and Clementina French. Three other children were christened: Henry James Williams, and Christine and Martha O'gilivie. Their parents' names are not listed. The 1850s saw a child to Thomas Latouche and Marina Williams, now Mrs and Mrs Thomas LaTouche; this family continued to live in Palmetto Grove.

There were marriages too. James Green, aged twenty-eight, and

Isabella Davis, twenty-three, of Rock Spring, got married in November 1872; so did Thomas Dixon, aged twenty-six, and Rebecca Meade, aged twenty, of Woodside. Neither of these two last names was on the list of slaves baptized into the Anglican faith, nor was the name Meade on the slave returns for Woodside Estate in 1817 and 1832, though Meade, as we later see, was one of those who got some of the Neilson land. Perhaps the Meades came into the area after emancipation and worked for the Neilsons.

It is through the list of taxpayers for the years 1869–82 found in the Government Archives at Spanish Town that we know who were the new owners of land in the greater Woodside area, thus we can keep track of the landholding history of the persons selected in the preceding chapter as potential ancestors.[3] This list tells us on what land and on what portion of land each person was paying taxes. These data tell us, though only for the first two years, the nature of landholding by the persons listed for the greater Woodside area. For the other years it is only possible to note how many acres of land persons listed had in their control, though the title of one such taxpayer – Lee – kept in his family today indicates that he did buy his land in 1881 for £7. All the others on the list could, like Lee, be owners of the land for which they pay taxes. We have no information for the first two years on Change Hill and Smailfield; for the latter, as well as Waterton, we had had no slave list in any case.

We see from the tax rolls that surnames we had selected from the baptismal slave list as ancestors do appear on these rolls. The ancestors for Louisiana had been Burnet/Burnett, Stanbury and Stewart. According to the data from the tax roll, only a Stanbury was able to secure land in this area where he had been a slave. A George Stanbury had two acres of this estate's land. Richards had been the sole ancestor selected for Palmetto Grove. A John Richards had one acre of land from that estate. In Richmond Hill the ancestral names had been Hamilton and Johnson. An Isaac Johnson by 1882 had managed to aquire twelve acres of the land on which he or his relatives had been slaves. In Woodside proper, the popular slave names had been Conie, Hamilton, Henry, Hermit/Hermitt, Neilson, Richards, Smith and Walker. Three Hamiltons – John, Stephen and W. – between them acquired nineteen-and-one-half acres; a Hermitt – James – had two acres. Frances Neilson's Alexander Sheriffe paid taxes on twelve acres of ex-Woodside plantation land, possibly the same on which they lived when they got married in 1842 and that was called Hopeton Content, according to their marriage certificate.[4] Thomas Richards held two Woodside acres in 1882, and there were several Walkers on the tax roll for 1882, including Richard Walker with six acres. Could this be Garrick alias Richard Walker, the sixteen-year-old creole slave whom Dr Neilson owned in 1817? Other Walkers were William with one acre and H.F. with ten.

For the Stapleton–Flemington–Braemar area, the ancestral names chosen had been Buchanan, Duncan and Timberlake. By 1869 a Buchanan – A. Buchanan – now owns one acre of land in Braemar, which he has in food provisions. There is no word on the landholding status of Duncan and Timberlake. There is no word either on our ancestor Harrison of Change Hill, but there is an Edwards who was a slave here in 1817–18 and we do find a John Edwards as a landholder in Change Hill in the 1880s. The enslaved Edwards was Margaret. A Margaret Edwards is a landholder in 1882 in Stapleton, and we find a Robert Edwards holding land in Louisiana at that time. Between 1817 and 1818 there was also a James Edwards enslaved on the Palmetto Grove plantation. In 1882 there is a John Edwards holding lands on that same plantation as a free man. Could this be the same John of Change Hill? The Johns, James and the two Margarets could well be related to each other by blood or by master. We have no word either on our ancestor Walker from Rock Spring. Hopewell's taxpayers were not listed, thus we have no word on the landed status of the ancestors carrying the names of Brown, Grant, Campbell, Douglas, Green, Gordon, Hamilton, Harris and Hudson for the period 1869–82.

Surnames of enslaved persons, other than those selected as ancestors, do appear on the tax roll for greater Woodside area in connection with the areas in which they were enslaved. E. Stanbury has six acres of land in Woodside proper where his or her family had been enslaved. So does Janet Morrison, who acquires one acre, Alex and Henry Grant, two acres each, and the Thomases, Blanche and William, who share the surname of a former slave and now, in 1882, have between them more than one hundred of Woodside proper's acres. We have reason to believe that these latter were offspring of Thomas, the former owner of Smailfield Estate. Slave names not selected as ancestors but appearing as taxpayers for the locations in which they were enslaved, exist for Palmetto Grove too. These names are Shaw, Lee and Thompson. Shaw has eight acres, with one each for Lee and Thompson; two Whites – Robert and James – have fifteen and two acres, respectively.

It could be that ex-slaves and their kin acquired lands on estates within greater Woodside but not in the areas in which they were enslaved. As we have suggested for the Edwardses above, so we suggest for Bennet. Robert Bennet has lands in Woodside proper. He could have been a Change Hill or Palmetto Grove Bennet stepping over the border to secure land here. He was a tenant and also an owner of land in Woodside proper. He owned five acres and was a tenant on one. Two acres were in ground provisions; the rest was ruinate. Robert Bennet called his property New Providence. Peggy Stewart shares a surname with one who had served on the Louisiana estates and could also have stepped over to Woodside for land. She has responsibility for nine acres, one of which she had in ground provisions in 1869; the rest was ruinate. She called her property Comfort Castle. The landholding Stewarts in Palmetto Grove and in Petersfield could also be her relatives by blood or master.

Burnet (Burnett) was a slave name on the Louisiana property. We find a Burnet holding land in neighbouring Richmond Hill in 1881–82. Did he too cross over to secure land? The Burnetts also held land in Woodside in 1882. There was an enslaved Lee on the Woodside proper estate in the days of slavery. Was he one of the family of Palmetto Grove Lees who held land in that area in the 1880s? African Jamaicans were accustomed during slavery to walk long miles from the slave quarters to their provision grounds. It is conceivable that a Woodside or Rock Spring Walker lived in 1882 where he had under slavery but held lands in the Stapleton–Braemar area, about two miles away. We find a Walker holding land in this Stapleton–Braemar area in 1882. It is quite possible that he was one of the line of the Rock Spring Walkers of slavery days who in 1882 lived in Rock Spring.

The Petersfield ancestors were Burnett, McDonald, White, Williams and Hibbert. There is no sign of the last four on the tax rolls for 1869–82 as holders of land in Petersfield, where they had been slaves; only Burnett appears. The success here is so phenomenal that we suspect a case of mistaken identity. In 1817 a Peter Burnett had been an enslaved person on the Petersfield estate. Could this be the Peter Burnett who, in 1870, was tenanting one acre of land in Petersfield on which he grows ground provisions? This Peter Burnett was also owner of Lucky Hill, part of what was formerly Decoy Estate. This is a large area. If the Peter Burnetts were one and the same, then that was a tremendous move.

Another Petersfield taxpaying name that had been on the slave list is Byfield. This name had not been popular enough for it to be isolated as an ancestor. However, a Byfield – M. Byfield – did manage to get lands on the estate on which he or she or his or her ancestors by blood or labour had been enslaved; another, R. Byfield, also had lands in neighbouring Palmetto Grove.

A new owner in Petersfield, the part that was once called Windsor Castle, is Philip Crossman. The Crossman name is no stranger to the list of enslaved people in the greater Woodside area, though it is in the adjacent Change Hill, not neighbouring Petersfield, that the records show them to have been bonded. In 1870 Philip was paying taxes on seven acres of land, only one of which was cultivated; the other six were in woodland. The Crossman family had owned lands in the southern part of greater Woodside as early as 1811, but the name does not appear at this time on the tax rolls for that area, Rock Spring; instead, we find Thomas Brown, William Lewis, Peter Rogers and William Thomas. These names were not on the list of baptized slaves for Rock Spring. The name Brown was, however, a popular one among the enslaved in nearby Hopewell. This Thomas Brown of Rock Spring owns one acre of land in ground provisions and has five acres in woods and ruinate. The surname Lewis follows a similar course: found on the Rock Spring list of taxpayers but on the Hopewell list of the baptized enslaved. There we had found an Ann-Maria and a Maria. It is a William Lewis, however, perhaps a relative of these women, whom we find holding land in nearby Rock Spring in 1869–82: he owns one acre in ground provision and two acres in woods and ruinate. Did these Hopewell slaves become the freemen of Rock Spring?

We have met the name Rogers before. There was a Sam Rogers who was the overseer on the Louisiana estate in 1838.[5] Is this Rogers, who in 1869 owned one acre of land in ground provisions, a blood relative of Sam, or a bondsman who was given his name? Rock Spring has another Thomas as a taxpayer. This one owns ten of Rock Spring's acres in 1870, one acre in ground provisions and the other nine in woods and ruinate. His identity is easy to guess. Along with his Rock Spring holding, he controls lands in Smailfield, one acre of which is in cane, one in coffee, eight in ground provisions and fifty-three in woods and ruinate.

Other such large acreages are held by other Thomases in Smailfield. This Thomas, and other large landholding Thomases of Woodside whom we have already met, are most likely the offspring of Robert Thomas, to whom Richard Thomas willed a part of his 328-acre Smailfield property in 1839.[6]

Other surnames which were on the list of baptized slaves and also appear as landholders in greater Woodside, not necessarily on the estates on which they were enslaved, are: Elizabeth Williams, Amy Williams, John Clarke, Alexander Green, Richard Gordon, Cecilia Lindsay, Edward Nelson and William Patterson. They got lands in Woodside proper. Thomas Murphy, a surname among the enslaved people of Change Hill, got lands in Petersfield, and a Catherine Johnson got lands in Stapleton.

The records for the late nineteenth century no longer speak of colour, so we cannot know from the official sources how many of the persons on the tax rolls, whose names or surnames were not on the slave list, are likely to have had a history of enslavement. It is to the oral sources that we turn, the fullest being for Woodside proper. Oral sources here advise us that a number of the persons on the tax rolls for the period 1869–82 were indeed black and formerly enslaved persons. Ismart Bogle and Henry Conridge are two of these.[7] In 1869 Ismart Bogle paid taxes on a piece of land which was formerly part of the Woodside property. He called this piece Happy Content. Ismart was not the only Bogle in Woodside. There was William as well. He called his properties Friendship and Pilgrim Hut. Henry Conridge was renting one acre of land in Hopewell by 1870, and was the owner of three of Woodside's acres. These latter he called Poor Man's Corner. Conridge had been in greater Woodside since 1856; this is the year in which his daughter Anne Elizabeth, born to his wife Selma in August of 1854, was baptized.[8]

The name Edmund/Edward Marshall (writing not clear) was one of those on the tax roll for the year 1869–70 but not on the list of baptized enslaved persons. Marshall controlled nine acres of what was formerly Woodside proper; one acre of this was in coffee and eight in woods and ruinate. His home was called Primrose Cottage. Though there was no sign of a Marshall as a surname in the baptismal slave lists for greater Woodside, we have met the name. It was associated with property in the greater Woodside area in 1824. In this year Samuel Murphy had charge of the property called Braemar on behalf of Jane Marshall. The name

Marshall has resonance closer home: it is the surname of the fiancé of
Helen Ismail, daughter of Mrs Jane Eliza Neilson and her husband, own-
ers of Woodside Estate. It is suggestive that a James Marshall, child of
Edward and Anne Evans, was baptized in Woodside in 1849. Was
Helen's husband a Marshall from Braemar who stayed on in Woodside
to pay taxes there and/or give his name to their children, and to servants
whose children pay taxes in the 1880s? More to the point, there was an
Edward John Marshall among Dr Neilson's slaves in 1817, listed in the
returns reproduced here. He was the four-year-old creole son of Mary
Ann Drew. Mary Ann, known as Fanny, was an African and only twenty-
three years old in 1817. Like her son, she was the property of Dr Neilson.
With Edward Marshall and the rest of her children, Mary Ann was
among the slaves transferred in 1829 to Mrs Neilson on the claim that
they were her private property. Is the difficult-to-decipher name
"Edward" and not "Edmund"? If this is so, then the son of Mary Ann
Drew has indeed, by 1870, turned into the proprietor of Primrose
Cottage, "part of Woodside".

Abraham Bartley was one of the post-emancipation owners of lands
in Woodside whose name is new to the area as far as the records available to us are concerned. He owned a part of Woodside, which he
called Spring Valley. It can be clearly seen on the map of 1880. There is
no evidence that he had been an enslaved person. Other new landholders in greater Woodside whose names were not on the slave list are:

James Cameron	Robert Hume	Sarah Hutton
Thomas Walsh	Maryam Willis	James Derry
George Gray	James Lumorsley	
Charles Lord	E.L. McCoomb	James Meade
George McKenzie	Ann Evans	Joseph Northover
Joseph Tucker	Thomas Prince	Alexander Panton
Adelaide Payne		
Robert Ryan	William Rose	Alex Rennicke
John D. Rose	Robert Stephenson	

With these new owners, 436 acres of the 734 acres of Woodside
proper, as it was in 1832, were gone out of the working hands of the
Neilsons — called Nelson on the map of 1880. Most of the new landholders whose names had not been on the list of slaves acquired acreages
far in excess of what was available to African Jamaicans under slavery.

The Thomases, as we have already pointed out, had more than one hundred acres; Ryan had thirty and three-quarters; William Ferguson, fifteen; Northover, twenty; Alex Rennicke (Ramiki), fourteen; Alexander Sheriffe, twelve, and Sarah Hutton, ten.

New landholders in Palmetto Grove, not seen on the list of slaves baptized into the Anglican faith, were: William Champany and R. Jones, Catherine Hunter, Hobalee*, John McKoy, T.W. Moore, Catherine Pecco, James Scrymger (name illegible), Elizabeth Stevens and William Treston. New landholders for Petersfield were: Charlotte Cox, Adeline Wallace, R. Murray and William Rose. For the Stapleton–Braemar area, they were: Elise Archibald, Timothy Hutton, Alexander Gillis; and for Louisiana: William Mouncer, Beckford and Anthony McClean, and Horatio Simmonds. As with Woodside proper, some of these new landholders had significant acreages. William Champany had 810 acres of the Palmetto Grove lands. Relatively large acreages also went to some whose surnames were on the slave baptismal list: to Martha Thomas, on whose possible siblings we have already commented, went sixty-five of Smailfield's, and to Charles Stewart went twelve.

Cultivating the land to feed oneself was nothing new to the newly freed African Jamaicans. During slavery, they had – males and females – been given a portion of land on the estate on which to grow their provisions.[9] In Jamaica it was the convention for these provision grounds to be some distance away from the estates' works and from the residences both of the enslaved work force and the masters' great house. The rationale behind this kind of allocation of space was that with their own fields far away, labour would serve its master totally until its free time came on the weekends, and with the Negro houses relatively close to the great house, the master could keep an eye on the workers. In the 1806 sketch of Waterton (see map 7), we see the great house across the road and the Negro houses and the works together; ruinate and Negro provision grounds are at the other end of the plantation. The Smailfield estate (see map 6) has the works near to the great house; we assume that the Negro houses would be close by. They were close to Rock Spring Estate. The Negro grounds abutted the Hamilton and Pollock land in what is today's Stapleton. The Waterton great house is very close to the border of the Change Hill estate. Its works and Negro houses and its ruinate and provision grounds are separated by land worked by Mr Neilson of Woodside. Was space consciously distributed so that a neighbour's farm or house was near to any convergence of the enslaved? Seems sensible.

The Neilsons must have followed this general pattern, for according to the oral sources they gave Bramber, a hilly area far from the great house but very close to the Louisiana and Waterton great houses, to the enslaved as their provision grounds.[10] This hillside was so sloped that it is possible from the Woodside great house to see people working there. Woodside's works, like so many others, was, we know from examining the ruins, close to a stream and close to the great house. If Woodside Estate follows the usual pattern, then the houses of the enslaved would be close to the great house and the works in an area today called Dryland. All of these are very close to the Rock Spring estate and very far from Bramber, the slave's provision grounds. Given these conditions the enslaved farmer here would have had a history of walking long distances from his home to his provision grounds, and the freedman would become accustomed to walking long distances to his field. The allotments given to the enslaved were not usually more than one-fifth of an acre; their new holdings were considerably more. Where were these holdings located? It is reasonable to assume that the space rented by the owners of failing estates to their ex-slaves would be where the slave allotments were.

The map of 1880 shows relatively large spaces where the names of the estates are. Further away from the names are smaller spaces divided into smaller parts. It is clear that the central area, quite likely the great house area, remains as the largest part of the old estate while the borders have been sold as lots. This is very clear in the cases of Palmetto Grove and Woodside proper. Evidently only the small parts at the edges of these plantations were alienated in 1880. Let us go back to the map of 1880 and look more closely at Woodside. Here we see "680:0:0" in the vicinity of the name "Woodside" and the words "small settlements" and "small lots" at the north-western boundary. This north-western boundary is the hillside of which Bramber, the former provision grounds for the enslaved, is a part. Slave provision grounds really became ex-slaves' farms, at least in the case of parts of greater Woodside.

We see that Woodside was, by the map of 1880, 680 acres. The Neilsons must have sold a total of thirty-four acres between 1832 and 1880 to Ismart Bogle, Robert Bennet, Henry Conridge, Edward Marshall and Peggy Stewart. Abraham Bartley, according to the register of taxes, held Spring Valley, "formerly Woodside". On the map of 1880, Spring Valley is marked as an area to the far east of the Woodside estate and was formerly called Pear Tree Grove. The Neilsons apparently sold the areas farthest from the Woodside great house area. Another alienated piece was that bounded by the roadside and touching Petersfield to the north-east. What happened to the plot encircled by Woodside lands that was sold in 1842 to Cousins? And now that some ex-slaves had such comparatively large amounts of what might have been their former provision grounds, there must have been some ex-slaves who were now without provision grounds. What was their source of livelihood?[11] Oral sources tell of barracks in which waged labourers lived in nearby estates such as Louisiana. This might have been their lot.

Shortly after emancipation, coffee growers in Jamaica moved towards the independent approach to the organization of labour;[12] the sum of jobs to be done was seen in terms of tasks, remunerations affixed to each and a time belt fixed in which the work should be completed. Workers were assigned tasks and left on their own to perform. Assuming that the estate owners in greater Woodside did this, some of the enslaved persons listed above are likely have been invited into these relatively responsible positions. It would have been advantageous for one of their kind, still favourably disposed towards the great house, to have had the job of liaising between workers and owners. According to oral accounts of his descendants, a Ferguson male had this job, being Mrs Neilson's headman during slavery and continuing to be close to her for the rest of her lifetime.[13] It is even claimed that her daughter, who lived across the road from him, had a child by him. Favourably disposed indeed![14]

No Ferguson name appears on the baptismal list for the Woodside estate between 1817 and 1834. It does, though, on the slave lists signed by Woodside's owner Dr Neilson in 1817 and 1820, as we can see from the slave returns for Woodside proper. The first person called Ferguson in the slave records consulted for Woodside Estate, is a Negro male. His name was Quamin, an African-sounding name; his alias was "William Ferguson". Quamin was born in Jamaica, possibly in Woodside, St Mary. His mother was Charlotte, born in Africa in 1762, and in 1817 one of Dr Neilson's slaves. She produced Quamin in about 1792, here in Jamaica. William Ferguson died in 1820 at age thirty-three, but there was at this time another Ferguson, Billy, who was only three years old. Billy's mother was Fanny alias Mary Ann Drew, who had also produced for Woodside the creole Edward John Marshall, four years earlier. Since there was no other Ferguson on the plantation, it is fair to assume that Billy was the son of William. As we have seen in another chapter, there were Fergusons in St Mary who owned Stirling Castle, and others who owned nothing but a few slaves.[15] There was also a Ferguson who was a surveyor in the parish in the late eighteenth century who could have owned the first black Ferguson and given this name to him or to his father.[16] Billy Ferguson – no doubt the William officially listed in the tax rolls for 1881–82, the sixty-three-year-old possible son of William, possible grandchild of Charlotte, all three generations slaves of the Neilsons – would be part of the Neilson history and inner circle. It is as Mrs Neilson's headman rather than Mr/Dr Neilson's headman that the Ferguson ancestor is remembered by his clan today.

It is in 1832, after the death of William John in 1828, that we find Mrs Jane Neilson listed as the official owner of slaves; she has thirteen slaves. The 1829 deposition of the executors of William John's estate, and her own deposition, now that she is a slave-owner, are revealing.[17] This document acknowledges the transfer of a number of slaves from the estate of Dr William John Neilson to his widow on the grounds that they had been her private possessions. Her own deposition admits to having one more than is transferred to her. The one name on her list that is missing from the transfer list is that of Billy Ferguson. Billy seems to have been Mrs Neilson's first slave, possibly specifically assigned to her by her dying husband.[18] The reports of the current Fergusons could be right: William Ferguson was well positioned to play liaison between the great house and its ex-slaves. So of course could his brother, Edward (Edmund?) John Marshall, the new master of Primrose Cottage.

Interestingly, it is from Ferguson's descendant, Mrs Leah Brisset, *née* Ferguson, that the kindest reports concerning Mrs Neilson have come down to us.[19] They credit Mrs Neilson with having given Bramber, an area near to today's Louisiana, to her slaves to grow their greens and collect water. Again, it is interesting that William Ferguson is one of the largest taxpayers on ex-Woodside land: he has fifteen acres. We surmise that a close and positive relationship with the former owners, and money saved from work with them, would have put an ex-slave such as Ferguson in a good position to use and eventually buy some of the lands that had formerly been provision grounds and were available for sale now that the owners no longer found agriculture in the area profitable. It is in this same Bramber area where the slave provision grounds are thought to have been that the Fergusons had, and today have, their lands.

In the list above for Palmetto Grove, we see the name "Hoobalee" distinguished by an asterisk. In the original records the word "coolie" is in brackets beside this name. This name and the associated description force us to note the coming of the East Indians into the area and their entry into land ownership. Hoobalee is one of the few Indian names mentioned in the records. We know from the oral sources, though, that there were several Indians in the greater Woodside area. They, like the Africans before them, had been subjected to name changes, as Eustace Brown, a descendant born in 1909, tells us.[20] They took names or were given names historically familiar to us, such as Dean, Grant, Brown, Edwards and Williams. Some Indian names survive: the Browns and Grants according to a descendant, Everald Brown, had had "Sammi" as their surname, and there is evidence from a land title in his possession, of "Jackoo" buying land in Woodside from "Mongorro".

Another descendant of the Browns, Busha Brown, tells us that "Mongorro" was a corruption of "Mangaree".[21] This land title, which is in the possession of Everald Brown, calls Jackoo and Mongorro "coolies".[22] This land is close to that of John Harmit, "Harmit" being the corrupted form of Hermit. The survey is done in the presence of Robert Brown, whom we know to have been formerly a Sammi, James Grant, also a Sammi, Manich and Hamiel. The last two are described as "coolies". Manich has been identified by Busha Brown as his grandfather. This sales agreement was granted in 1898, at the close of the century, at which time those whose lands abut yours are the ones called to witness the survey of the land mentioned in the sales contract. Apart from John Hermit, all the parties related to this piece of Woodside land in 1898 were Indians. This property was close to where the great house and works were, and where the slave houses would have been.

The propensity of former slaves to work on their own plots and to give their time to estates only when they felt like, led their former masters to seek other sources of labour. Europeans were imported but they failed to fill the bill. Indians were tried. Their migration began in 1845 and continued in spurts until 1917. The first arrivants seemed to have been dispatched to estates in batches of twenty.[23] They were to serve for five years, were paid a daily wage, and were to be given free passage back to India or a cash bounty to settle here as ordinary citizens, should they wish to do so at the end of this period. In 1860 the stipendiary magistracy was resuscitated and eight of the old magistrates were commissioned to see to the care of the Indians.[24] Alexander Gordon Fyfe was one of those brought back into helping another group of people to settle into the Jamaican society. He was now an immigration sub-agent, in charge, as before, of an area that included St Mary and its adjoining parish – Metcalfe and St George, later to be merged into St Mary. "Is him bring the slave dem come here," says his descendant, John Fyffe.[25]

In this part of Jamaica there is no distinction made between slavery and indentured labour, as the Indian service was officially called. Everald Brown, a descendant of Indians, speaks of his ancestors as having come here "through the slavery business".[26] Fyfe's descendant continues, in reference to Alexander Gordon Fyfe, whom he calls "Captain Fyfe": "Him used to take care of the slave dem at Station [the ruins of the Woodside estate's works]".[27] It is very likely that Fyfe, who at the same time was also inspector of the island prisons and had continued to be a magistrate in the petty sessions, did have a "station" in greater Woodside, in which he did the several things he had to do with persons, including Indians.

According to Eustace Brown, interviewed at age eighty-five, his grandfather originally came from India, served elsewhere in Jamaica, then with his wife found their way to Palmetto Grove.[28] There they were involved in a land deal with another Indian – Dean. A Dean, as we know, was the proprietor of a part of Palmetto Grove. It is very likely that this Indian man was Dean's worker and that he took or was given his name. Both families, Dean and Brown, subsequently settled in Woodside. Brown's children were Robert, David, Charles, George, Elizabeth and James. Oral sources agree that one and possibly two of these children – George and Elizabeth – were a part of Mrs Neilson's household as "school boy" and "school girl", terms which translate to mean apprentices.[29] Did Eustace's grandfather, the father of Robert, David, Charles, George, Elizabeth and James, come to greater Woodside as indentured labour, under the security of Mr Fyfe? George was subsequently given an acre of land near to the great house, apparently by the Neilsons for whom he had worked.[30] Shortly after, the property moved out of the hands of the Neilson family and he was asked by a Mr Johnnie, possibly the William John who was legally to succeed to the estate after the death of George William, to surrender this one acre for five acres fur-

ther away in the area called Dryland, an area that seems to have been
the residences of the enslaved labourers of the estate and in which the
"coolies" – Jackoo, Mangaree, Manich and Hamiel – owned lands in
1898.[31] With the gift of land to George, a Sammi, apparently began the
ascendancy of the Indians in that section of Woodside called Dryland.
The influence was more than a landed one: George Brown, remembered today as "Capry" (apparently a corruption of "corporal"), also
took over the station.

The ex-slave family Hermit was a large owner in that area as well.
Their name appears in the list of those slaves belonging to the Woodside
estate and baptized into the Anglican faith between 1817 and 1834. The
name has been in the area longer than that: in 1809 the Neilson's land
is described as abutting that of Patience Hermit.[32] We note too this surname among those of property owners, and in the list of those who could
have made their livelihood from the sale of their slaves' labour.[33] No
Hermitt was among Dr Neilson's slaves in 1817–23 or among those of
his mother Frances for the corresponding period, but we find that a
young Negro woman named Pamela Cunningham, owned by Dr
Neilson, gave birth to two children surnamed Hermit in 1825 and
1827;[34] these were Donald and Jacket and their names were on the
baptismal list. A Charles Hermit was on this list too. He was not named
in the Neilson's 1829 slave returns, and was clearly born between that
date and 1831. These children and their mother were not in Widow
Neilson's private collection, as were no doubt her household slaves. They
would have been field slaves, but not for very long, since by 1838,
when they were between nine and thirteen, they would have been freed.
To do what?

These black Hermits' father, given three births to this one unusual
name, could have been in a steady and responsible relationship with their
mother. This is very possible, if the father is Robert Hermit, thirty-six
years old at the time of the birth of the eldest, a man who is described
in his owner, Patience Hermit's deposition of 1817, as a "Christian".
As such, he would be given to monogamy and paternal responsibility.[35]
Patience Hermit's deposition was signed before William John Neilson
in August of 1817, X-ed really, for Patience was illiterate. If Donald,
Jacket and Charles were the children of Robert Hermit of Patience
Hermit's Carpenter's Hut, a woman known to William John Neilson of
Woodside, they would perhaps have a choice after emancipation in 1838,

of labouring on Mrs Neilson's coffee estate and/or learning carpentry from their father, who is likely to have learned it from the owners of Carpenter's Hut, his masters. Work at a skill like carpentry would have given them ready cash to save and eventually buy lands from Mrs Neilson. There is documentary as well as oral evidence that the Hermits/ Hermitts were significant landowners in nineteenth-century and early-twentieth-century Woodside.

Mrs Vie Campbell, *née* Hermitt, born about 1912, and Leonard Hermitt, born 1919, say that a Charles Hermit was their grandfather. This Charles could be the one born after 1829 and before 1831, or his son or nephew, for there is definitely another and younger Charles in the generation between the Charles of 1829–31 and Mrs Campbell's grandfather.[36] The recognized grandfather had several nephews – John, James, Theophilus, Walter, and Robert, possibly children of his older brothers Donald and Jacket. As we have seen, a James Hermit (Harmit) is listed among those paying taxes on Woodside land in 1880–81. According to a title in the possession of the Brown family, a John M. Hermit owned land in the part of Woodside called Dryland in 1898, and according to a title in the possession of the Renikie/Ramikis, Jacob owned lands there too, in 1903.[37]

Charles's granddaughter knew him to own, in the early twentieth century, six pieces of Woodside land – Bottom Yard, Want, Madden Field, Bennet Land – possibly bought from the Bennet who had owned part of Woodside in 1869 – Neilson and Tun. This granddaughter knows of a larger Hermitt clan who owned lands in Dryland, which they called Hermitage.[38] Undated documentary evidence shows a John to have bought eighteen acres of land formerly in Woodside, bordered by the road to Port Maria.[39] Oral sources have been able to identify this piece of land. Robert bought a piece nearby where "Mrs Neilson's daughter" lived, according to Mr Levi Hudson and Mrs Leah Brisset, *née* Ferguson. Robert and James are said to have been "sent", according to the report of the widow of John Hermitt, son of John Hermit, to Palmetto Grove where their father had bought lands for them.[40] John the first was given control of some parts of Dryland.

Charles's grandchildren called him "tata", a word appearing, as we have seen, in many African languages, as a way of addressing fathers and other venerated older men.[41] This Charles also practised polygamy, having a wife at Top Yard and a concubine at Bottom Yard.[42] The lands mentioned as controlled by Charles carry no suggestion that his wife and/or concubine were part owners of these lands, or that he worked lands which were theirs. The review of landholders for the greater Woodside area finds few women on the list. Those for Windsor Castle are Sarah Forbes, Carolyn Morgan and Rebecca Darling – three out of forty-eight new landholders. The disparity was not as stark for the rest of the area as a whole. About one fifth of the new landholders on the tax roll between 1869 and 1882 were women. They were: Ann Evans, Sarah Hutton, Cecilia Lindsay, Janet Morrison, Adelaide Payne, Peggy Stewart, Blanche Thomas, Amy Williams, Elizabeth Williams and Maryam Willis. These ladies had lands in Woodside proper. Elise Archibald and Margaret Edwards acquired lands in Stapleton; and Catherine Hunter, Catherine Pecco and Elizabeth Stevens got lands in Palmetto Grove, according to the tax rolls. There was one woman listed for Petersfield, Adeline Wallace, and one for Smailfield, Martha Thomas. Given this low level of ownership of the major economic asset in the culture, the women of greater Woodside, including Charles Hermitt's wife and concubine, would need economic as well as emotional and sexual succour from the men around them.

The Jamaican government was not very good about repatriating the first Indians who came.[43] It could have been a breach of faith that kept the Sammis, now Browns, here; it could be choice. Whatever the reason, the lump sum given to them at the end of their five-year indentured service would have been available to them for investment in land. The failing coffee and sugar estates of greater Woodside might have attracted them as labourers, and the owner might have been willing to give them first option when there was land available for sale; they might have been required to do so by the terms of their indenture. The Browns, ensconced in Dryland, intermarried with the Grants, another family with roots in India. These are said to have come into Woodside from the parish of St Ann, and one of them, James, is said to have been a "school boy" in the Neilson household.[44] Born in 1857 and dying sixty-two years later,[45] James married Elizabeth Brown, the "school girl" in the Neilson household. We note that he was one of the interested parties in the survey of land to be passed between "Jackoo (coolie)" and "Mongorro (coolie)".[46]

The Grants subsequently controlled a vast area of the Woodside property situated below Dryland, bordering on Richmond Hill and close to Stapleton, as well as lands in the Rock Spring–John Crow Spring–Jumper area. Their association with the Neilson family must have been instrumental in effecting the initial transfer of lands. The issue of Elizabeth Brown and James Grant, the reputed "school girl" and one of the "school boys" to the Neilson family, married with the Timberlakes of Stapleton.[47] A Brown married an Aitkin, one of whom was listed among the slaves on the Palmetto Grove plantation. The Aitkin who married into the Brown family is said by their descendants to have been the child of a Scottish plantation owner and a black slave. Is this Aitkin-Brown of the same family as that of the slave on the Palmetto Grove plantation named Mary Aitkin? Aitkin joined with the Browns into subsequent ownership of great portions of the southern part of Woodside, the area from Dryland to the St Catherine/St Mary border, called today, Aitkin Town.

The Browns also married into families which could have been those of the former slaves – Charles Brown married a Shaw and James Brown, a Walker. One of James's sons was named James. This son, the "Manich", mentioned above, married into the Coleman family. The descendants of this union claim the original Woodside Coleman to have been the offshoot of a Scotsman who owned property in the St Mary/St Andrew area. The catalogue of maps in the National Library of Jamaica does carry a diagram of a patent of three hundred acres of land to a Henry Coleman;[48] no date is given. Could this be the ancestor of the Woodside Colemans into whom the Browns married? There is mention also in 1840 of a Jane Collman as the postmistress of the office that continues to serve the greater Woodside area today, the Pear Tree Grove post office.[49] Is Collman a corruption of Coleman? We do know from a title in the possession of the Browns that a Robert Coleman owned lands in the Dryland part of Woodside in 1894.

The Indians moved into the twentieth century as, for the most part, a genetically creolized group living in a particular part of Woodside that stretched from the area immediately below the great house to its southernmost extreme. Their establishment in the area put two sets of Browns in the greater Woodside area as well as two sets of Grants, for as we have seen there were Browns and Grants in the slave population, particularly in Hopewell, years before the Indians came into the areas.

Planters also tried labourers from Africa. Sierra Leone was the major source. By 1842, 1,270 Africans had arrived.[50] After 1843 more came from Sierra Leone and from St Helena. A ship, the *Herald,* carrying

Sierra Leoneans, had docked at Port Maria in 1841. Twenty St Mary estates took these workers. Westmoreland's estate in Metcalfe was one of the biggest takers. The stipendiary magistrate for the area wrote of these Africans who had come on this ship and lived in Metcalfe, that the planters were happy with them; that most could read and a few could write; that they were "of a higher degree of civilisation than the generality of our black population".[51] Not everyone was as delighted with them. Henry Pupley, an immigration agent, writing from nearby Pear Tree Grove, St Mary, states that the immigrants brought by the *Herald,* with the exception of twenty-seven, would not enter into any work agreement, though many good offers had been made to them.[52] Their excuse was that they wanted to see the country first. The good officer felt that this off-hand attitude was due to the fact that monetary advances had been sent to the migrants. This they kept until their entry into Jamaica, used as subsistence here, and would not work until it was finished.

These new Africans, like the Indians, came to Jamaica with the understanding that they would work at a low salary for a number of years with one estate and then, with a lump sum in hand, either stay to become Jamaicans or go back home with passage paid by the Government of Jamaica. Alexander Rennicke – this surname sometimes written as Remique, as Remichie and earliest as Ramiki and Ramakee – a landowner in Woodside since 1854, could have been one of those Sierra Leoneans who came over from Africa, more "civilized" than other blacks in the population, Africans who treated the immigration agent in a decidedly off-hand way.[53] Ramiki was a resident of Metcalfe when he bought his first piece of land in greater Woodside. He could have been one of those new Africans who eventually settled down to work on an estate. The land he bought was situated in Rock Spring. His lump sum could have helped him to buy the further fourteen acres in Woodside that he had acquired by 1881. Remikie/Ramiki descendants say they have always known that they came from "somewhere else" and have been trying to identify that "somewhere".[54]

Internal migration brought others into Woodside to become landowners paying taxes in 1881–82. Hugh Walker, possibly H.F. Walker of the tax roll, was one of these. Hugh Walker had been a slave on an estate in St Ann.[55] He found his way over to Woodside where he bought lands and married into the Forbes family.[56] His entry meant that there were now two unrelated strands of Walkers in the area; even two Hugh

Walkers, for one was born to the Woodside estate in 1820 to Selina Montague, the lady who ought to have been freed by the terms of Dr William John Neilson's 1828 will.[57] Which of the ones paying taxes in 1881–82 was the immigrant and which the native?

Another family coming in from St Ann in the later part of the nineteenth century, and having a surname that appeared during slavery as well as in the tax list for 1881–82, was the Williams family. One of these Williamses produced a son in 1850 by a second marriage to a Smith from Richmond and bought lands in the Rock Spring–Smailfield area, close to Richmond.[58] Like the Walkers, there were now two sets of Williamses in the greater Woodside area, as there were two sets of Browns and Grants. There also seems to have been, by the turn of the twentieth century, other Forbeses besides those descended from the ones baptized in Hopewell and Woodside between 1817 and 1831.

What social structure and what culture emerged as peculiar to Woodside out of the behaviour of these new residents and new landowners, who now joined residents and landowners whose forebears had experienced slavery in or close to the areas in which they now had their homes and fields?

Chapter 7

Institutions and Their Development in Woodside, *circa* 1833–1948

Reverend John Chandler of the Baptist Church in Jamaica noted with obvious jealousy in 1841 the economic advantages which the Anglican clergy had over priests of other denominations. He reported that there were twenty-one incumbents and twenty-one curates in Jamaica, the former receiving £500 plus glebe; that the curates got £400 each; that six ministers were supported by the home government and nineteen were paid out of parish funds, and that there were seventy-six Church of England ministers. Chandler's jealousy continues: "Annual income derived by the clergy from parish taxes, island chest, the glebe lands and slave compensation money including salaries paid to bishops and archdeacons amounts to about £40,000 and the House of Assembly proposed to double the number of island curates."[1]

The Jamaican government, dominated by slave holders, had reviewed and amended the laws relating to the Anglican clergy since 1833 so that they would be more involved with the population that was about to be emancipated. Rectors and curates were now to allow slaves to be married in the holy places of the Anglican Church provided that there was consent in writing from their masters.[2] The establishment offered economic inducements to the clergy for working among the ex-slave population, setting in train the prerequisites for attracting more clerics of this faith into the control of the socialization of newly freed people. The plan worked. There certainly was an Anglican presence in the form of the island curate ministering in the greater Woodside area when Henrietta Morrison and Thomas Downs, among other enslaved persons, were joined in holy matrimony.[3] This was the Reverend Archer who lived in Rock Spring and died in 1841.[4]

There is no documentary word after 1831 on the Baptist presence at Brae Head which had engaged the slaves. A cornerstone dated 1880 is evidence that a church of this faith was built at Richmond Hill in the southernmost end of greater Woodside.[5] We know, too, that by 1842 the Anglicans had competition in the form of the Jamaica Missionary Presbytery that was established at Carron Hall, a district very near to Petersfield and to Brae Head.[6] It could be that the Baptists of Brae Head had not recuperated from the burning of their mother church in Port Maria in the mid-1830s and had transferred to the Presbyterians. The growth of the Presbyterian Church notwithstanding, and despite the possible existence of the Baptist Church at Brae Head, people from areas near to Carron Hall such as Petersfield and nearby Palmetto Grove continued to have their children christened in the Anglican Church. They even came from Carron Hall itself. In 1850 William Kelly (no parents mentioned) eighteen months old, of Carron Hall, was baptized at Woodside. Reverend Davidson, the island curate in 1849 and the Reverend Edwards after him, did a great deal of baptizing and up until the late 1860s burying of residents of the Petersfield area.[7] Along with the curate, a missionary catechist was working in the area on behalf of the church in 1883 and in 1887 there was a district catechist. The former position was held by R.H. Pusey and the latter by W.M.L. Miles.[8]

Most of the people who married in the Anglican faith, those who baptized their children in this faith and those who were buried in this faith, were labourers. The Anglican Church in the greater Woodside area was, at this stage, missionary to the blacks as well the few whites left in the area, to whom they had initially ministered, and the few middle class people who had stayed on. One of the few non-labourers using the Woodside church was Robert Green of Smailfield, who in 1846, with Mary Bennet, produced a child whom they baptized at the Woodside church.[9] Green was a carpenter, the most popular non-labouring profession among those using the church. Thomas Latouche of Palmetto Grove, who produced a child by Marina Williams whom he later married, was also carpenter; so was Joseph Hutton of Stapleton, who in 1849 had produced a child by Diana Thompson. William Dixon of Hopewell, who produced Henrietta Dixon by his wife Clarissa in 1848, was also a carpenter associated with the church.

According to the oral and written reports, the Baptist church was taken over by the Anglicans; the reports do not say when. They also state that the Anglican church was at first at a place called Khouriland.[10] This Khouriland is between Petersfield and Woodside proper, close to Palmetto Grove and within easy walking distance of Rock Spring, Smailfield, Louisiana, Waterton and Windsor Castle. Khouriland is adjacent to Brae Head, the site of the 1831 Baptist church. The Reverend Bayliss, in discussing this Brae Head church,[11] had said in 1831 that it was much too small and that the people were building themselves a new one. Perhaps the Baptists did build themselves a bigger church after all, and passed this on to the Anglicans, for the church in which the 1876 successors of the Reverend Davidson administered the sacraments could hold 250 people.[12] It did not reach this limit for any normal church service up to the end of the nineteenth century, when it was moved to its present site; nor was the number of members anywhere near this figure in the twentieth century, the highest being the 127 for 1925. In 1941 it was only 96, perhaps facing competition from the Seventh-Day Adventists and the Salvation Army. There are no other figures available for twentieth-century membership.

The church attendance for the years for which we have these data – 1876 and 1898 – was seventy and forty-five respectively. In 1893, two years after the church moved to its present site, it had one hundred members, and in 1898 this number had fallen to seventy-five.[13] Celebrants of holy communion were few: in 1898 there were just ten. Marriages were also few: eight in 1876, one in 1893 and two in 1898. Baptisms in the Anglican faith were usually of children, though baptism of adults did take place, as in the case of Henry John, an African adult who was baptized in 1855 in the Highgate church, the mother of the Woodside church. Baptisms, which we assume to be of children, were relatively frequent, being sixty in 1876 and forty in 1893. By 1893 the church was operating a day school as well as a Sunday school. On roll for the Sunday school were thirty-two children in 1876, fifty-two in 1893 and sixty in 1898. The average attendance in 1893 was thirty and in 1898, forty-five. The day school, on the other hand, had 120 on roll in 1893 and

126 in 1898, with an average attendance in 1893 of 80 and of 65 in 1898.

The Anglicans' most consistent clients were evidently children to be baptized and children to be educated. Restated from the perspective of the freedman or freeman, the Anglican Church existed to equip his children for life in the English culture. Meanwhile, he practised what of this culture his economic status allowed. Like his old master, he gave his home a name – Friendship, Pilgrim's Hut and Happy Content for the Bogles paying taxes and owning lands in Woodside in 1869–70; New Providence for Robert Bennet; Poor Man's Corner for the Conridges, Primrose Cottage for the Marshalls, and Comfort Castle for Peggy Stewart.[14]

Alongside this Anglicanism was Afro-oriented behaviour retained from that brought over with the enslaved population or introduced by the new Africans who settled in Metcalfe. Hopewell was listed as being in Metcalfe; it could have had new Africans: it certainly, in the 1820s, had people who had been born in Africa.[15] The Africans, new or old, practised in greater Woodside, of which Hopewell is a part as defined in the introduction, the *manalva* which, in the way the drum is beaten and its emphasis on the protection of the queen, looks very much like the presentation of the kings and queens in the durbar of the peoples of West Africa.[16] West African emphasis on metaphysics was here too. A member of the Bogle family is remembered and recorded in Martha Beckwith's *Black Roadways* as a very effective Myal man living in Woodside.[17] Bogle, according to Beckwith's account, wore wooden hoops in his ears to distinguish him as a professional.

One of the Walkers of Rock Spring, a name which indicates that he could have been one of the slaves or a descendant of one of the slaves on that plantation, wore similarly distinguishing paraphernalia, bracelets and necklaces, and he used the rattle drum and big drum. Walker advertised himself as having extrasensory powers.[18] People in Rock Spring, this part of greater Woodside where the Anglican Reverend Archer had lived until 1841 and where the stipendiary magistrate Fyfe had a residence, kept or brought with them into the area their parents' memories of their ancestors' memories of Africa, memories of them "dancing" the treadmill and singing "bantu" songs to calm their nerves, to the great amusement of the whites in the great house.[19] The Anglicans were not able to totally institute the nuclear family in this area: Charles Hermitt

– Tata – of Woodside, as we have seen in the preceding chapter, maintained in public view a polygamous union that recalls Africa – he had one wife and family at Bottom Yard and one at Top Yard.

Membership in the Anglican church rose steadily, however, from the beginning of the twentieth century to the middle of its second decade, even if attendance did not. In 1907 membership was 110, increasing by thirty-five from the 1898 figure. In 1911 it had increased again by twelve to 122, and by 1925 the church had 127 members.[20] Four years later, in 1929, it ceased to be a mission station and graduated into a full-fledged church. By this time it has received its gift of the old Woodside great house, and after the destruction of its own building by the hurricane of 1891 it had moved to the centre of Woodside proper.[21] Years of effort led to the transformation of the great house into a church. This effort itself led to the destruction of the stone work defining the immediate environs of the Woodside great house, for it was these stones that it used to extend itself.

Though the figure for membership increased in the early twentieth century, the figure for baptisms was surprisingly less than it had been in the earlier period. For 1907, it was thirty-three, seven less than it had been in 1898 and it was even less in 1911, being only twenty-five.[22] The number of celebrants of communion rose from ten in 1898 to thirty in 1907. The Sunday school and the day school increased their numbers, both of those on roll and the average number of those attending. The 1898 figure of forty-five for average Sunday school attendance increased in 1911 by thirteen to fifty-eight, and the number on roll increased from sixty in this time period to ninety-nine. It fell again to forty-four in 1925. The number on roll fell too, to eighty-four from ninety-nine. The day school suffered a similar fluctuation. On roll in 1911 were 215 students, an increase over the 1898 figure of 126, but this figure fell to 188 in 1925.

The tapering off of the figures for actual school attendance was less dramatic. The figure for 1898 had been sixty-five, fifteen less than the 1893 figure. By 1911 this figure had more than doubled to 136. In 1925 it was one less. The gap between the numbers actually attending school and those on roll had fallen. The ratio had been in 1893, 80:120; in 1898, 65:126; in 1911, 136:215 and in 1925, 135:188. The decline in the baptism figures mentioned above would indicate that fewer people wanted their children to be a part of the Anglican faith; that there is no accompanying decrease in the figures for the day school attendance, and that the numbers of those taking communion rose, indicate that those who enrolled their children in school in 1925 were serious about keeping them there, and that those who were already Anglicans were serious about being so. Mr Vernal Kelly, whose definition of the boundary of Woodside began this work, was one of the students here at this time, and one of those who attended the church and its Sunday school.

The elementary school was kept in the church building and the cleric of the church was the manager of the school. This clergyman lived outside of the area. The district catechist and missionary catechists mentioned above also lived outside of the area. The headmaster, who eventually took over the job of district catechist, was an import, though Jamaican, so were the assistant teachers. This twin entity, the church/school, which was the most public and facilitating institution in the area, was dominated apparently by Jamaicans born and raised outside of greater Woodside.

Analysis of the school registers for the period 1928–48 tells us that the people in greater Woodside who were most active in this church were among the most numerically significant families in the area and among those whose families had been long resident here, though not all of the latter were active church members. We have used frequency of surnames in the school register as the measure of numerical significance.

An examination of these 1928–48 registers allows us to see which families were numerically dominant in the area. The ten surnames most frequently seen in these records are, in descending order: the Browns, the Walkers, the Edwardses, the Grants, the Hamiltons, the Williamses, the Hermitts, the Thomases, the Stanburys and the Morrisons. All these names were among those listed in the slave baptism records for 1817–34. We know that there were two sets of Browns, Walkers and Grants. There were also two sets of Morrisons, one coming into the area in the 1920s. It is tempting to conclude that these frequently seen names on the school register between 1928 and 1948 were descendants of persons who had been here since slavery. Of these, the Walkers, the Browns, the Grants and the Williamses are reported to have been early members of the church.[23] We know, however, from oral reports, that the Browns and Grants mentioned here are those genetically mixed with the Indians who arrived here after emancipation. We hear, too, that the Walkers and the Williamses who were involved with the church are those who came into the area in the 1850s and 1860s. Two Walker brothers from this later arriving family, we are also told, held the important positions of people's warden and minister's warden in the early-twentieth-century life of the Anglican church in Woodside.[24] A significant proportion, then, of this group that was so involved with the development of the area – the church/school – was, in the twentieth century, led by first- and second-generation residents of the area, persons who had a parent or grandparent born outside of the greater Woodside area.

There were other families besides these first- and second-generation residents of Woodside – these migrants or half-migrants to the area – who were firmly established in the Anglican Church in the twentieth century. Some are names known to the slave list and baptismal list for Woodside proper, as well as the lists of slave-owners in greater Woodside and in the parish of St Mary. Such names also appear in the school registers, but not as frequently as those mentioned in the preceding paragraph. These were Pattersons, Leslies, Wrights, Kellys. Not seen on pre-emancipation lists for the area or the parish, but said by Mrs Gladys Walker, author of the first published history of the Woodside church, to be "early families who contributed to the development" of the church, are people with the names McKoy, Barclay and Cowan.[25] Add to this the name Conridge, which appeared in the 1850s on the baptismal list and on the list of taxpayers of the 1860s to 1880s and whom we know from personal experience and oral reports to have survived to be the beadle of the Anglican church in the early to mid-twentieth century. The Conridges, if we go by the school registers, did not produce male offspring who stayed in the village. The name McKoy is similarly under-represented on the school registers. It appears in the list of taxpayers for Palmetto Grove; McKoys were obviously here in the 1880s. There are very few of them, however, on the school registers between 1928 and 1948. There is no sign of the Barclays and Cowans. They could even have been post-1880 imports.

There were, too, names familiar from the baptismal slave list for the greater Woodside area that are found among the school-going population but not mentioned as stalwarts of the church. The most frequently seen of these are the Andersons, the Clarkes, the Johnsons, the Hudsons, the Redwoods, the Jameses, the Stewarts, the Forbeses, the Whites and the Campbells. There are still others, found on the baptismal slave lists for Woodside proper and greater Woodside, but in low numbers on the school lists and not at all on the lists of early members of the Anglican church. Among these are McKenzie, Bolt, Burnett, Aitkin, Mitchell, Lee, Green, Ogilive, Buchanan. The foregoing indicates that as far as the continuity of families was concerned, there was a considerable degree of stability from the slavery days to the early days of the twentieth century. Woodside people were, however, the foregoing also indicates, selective in their acceptance of the church/school coalition, accepting the Anglicans' gift of schooling more often than their gift of religion.

The greater Woodside area, between 1799 and 1838, had been a place in which families presided over agro-businesses that involved large groups of enslaved, resident labour. Neighbours saw each other as serious proprietors, doing business with each other by due process of law, even within families, as happened when Frances Neilson made William Neilson responsible for the property of her young son. The arrangement, as we saw in an earlier chapter, was ratified by law. The law, the Vestry and the House of Assembly governed the lives of these early-nineteenth-century Woodside people. Medical doctors lived among them; slave traders in the internal market, financiers, lawyers and, latterly, clergymen and civil servants too. They made arrangements for their defence. Most were officers in the militia. The emancipation and the freedom given to the enslaved population brought changes to this unilinear, interlocking system: they made it into a high motility, many-faceted one. We have only to look at the faces of those people who are now the Woodside people to see this "manyness", and at the school registers to see the high degree of continuous shifting in and out. New Africans, like Indians, brought their culture to make two strains of Africanisms, to add a dash of Asian styles and to increase the cultural "manyness" of the area.

One of the things that emancipation brought was a freedom of movement of the former work force. This changed the economic as well as the visual picture of the area. After emancipation, black people could move as they wished from one place to the other, from one perceived advantage to another. An economy that had depended on their immobility had to seek other forms of labour. Because of this gift of motion that mandated the importation of other workers, Jamaica began to see Indian faces and behaviour, as well as new African faces and behaviour. After their five-year indenture, these new people were allowed geographic mobility. Their exercise of this freedom brought them into greater Woodside by the 1860s, and brought to Woodside other skin shades, hair quality and cultural foci.

The whites' admission of their failure to make their former coffee and sugar plantations profitable, as we have already discussed, made lands available to these new African and Asian immigrants, as well as to the landless ex-slaves who had stayed on or who had migrated into the area. The parish of St Ann was a major sender of ex-slaves to the area. The later Walkers and Williamses came from this parish in the 1860s; so did the Indian Grants and the coloured Paynes and Rhyons. Another wave of migrants came in the 1880s. Banana had by then been identified as an economic crop capable of being grown on a large scale. It was touted as a crop that could take the economic place of coffee and sugar. Large tracts of land that had resisted the importunities of the land-hungry ex-slaves, Indians and new Africans were now made available to the wealthy: Hopewell Estate went to John Pringle, all 1,793 acres of it.[26]

For whatever reason, clergymen were among those making these large purchases. In 1882, when Hopewell passed to John Pringle, Reverend Henry Scott took 810 acres of Palmetto Grove land and he and his family, like Pringle, held onto it for a great deal of the next century. Pringle was a doctor employed by the government. It was quite usual, according to Veront Satchell, for land of such size to be taken by such professionals, and it does seem, in the case of greater Woodside, by government affiliates and lawyers.[27] Woodside proper and parts of Louisiana went to T.J. Cawley, a lawyer and contender for a seat in the Legislative Council. Another part of Woodside proper went to a clergyman, the Reverend Mitchell. It was from these two men that some of those who had come into greater Woodside in the 1860s, such as the Walkers, got lands.[28]

If the James Gayleard of St Catherine, from whom the Ramikis bought a parcel of Rock Spring land in 1854,[29] was the Honourable James Gayleard, chief justice of Jamaica in 1833, then the practice of passing of lands in the greater Woodside area to government-affiliated professionals was not a late-nineteenth-century phenomenon. Rock Spring's association with agents of government went even further back than this possible ownership by the chief justice, and forward as well. After the tenure of the Burrowes, by 1840 Rock Spring had fallen into the hands of Alexander Cooke, government physician, vestryman and later member of the Assembly for St Mary.[30] In the early twentieth century it fell into the hands of the Honourable W. McNeil, the representative of St Catherine to the Legislative Council.[31]

The 1880s takeover of large tracts in greater Woodside had meant the creation of banana plantations and jobs. This attracted labourers. Others followed, to build the houses they and the new middle class of black Anglican peasants would need. Among these was the father of Nathan Toomer.[32] Forced out of Clarendon by persistent drought, he came in, to become the master carpenter in greater Woodside. The Toomers subsequently married into the long-standing Stanbury family, into which the later Browns had also married. Banana and the good price it fetched helped to differentiate the ex-slave and ex-indentured workers into middle class and labouring class, a differentiation which, with the arrival of one such as Nathan Toomer, could be expressed in the nature of one's dwelling.

Later arrivals into the area were the phenotypically and culturally distinct Lebanese and the Chinese – the Khouris, the Lazaruses and a Chinese family with the name Wilson, among others. The Lebanese became landholders, renting rather than farming, and, like the Chinese, shopkeepers. By the time the Lebanese arrived in the greater Woodside area, the Greek Orthodox Church to which many belonged in their own country, had become united "in communion" with the Church of England, of which the Anglican Church in Jamaica was a part.[33] The Lebanese, now landholders and members of the dominant church, merged with the village culture in more ways than one, for they produced children by the natives. They did not change their names, as black people had had done to them and as had happened with some Indians and Chinese in the area. Thus the school registers carry the occasional Lebanese name – George and Maggaido – a few spots take on Lebanese names such as Khouriland, and some more brown-skinned children joined the black children playing at recess time. The Lebanese and Chinese were the shopkeepers, the latter dealing in grocery items and, at least in Woodside, also produce, buying the farmers' cacao for resale in Kingston. The Lebanese were principally dry goods merchants but also entered other areas of commerce. A female Khouri – Enid – had a shop as well as a gas station in nearby Carron Hall in the early part of the twentieth century.[34]

The Chinese were generally less integrated into the culture of the areas of Jamaica which received them, although as grocers and produce-dealers they were in daily face-to-face relationships with the mass of the people. Strained relationships between them and the African-Jamaican population throughout southern and eastern Jamaica led to anti-Chinese riots, locally called "Chiney looting". Woodside was one of several villages in Jamaica that saw anti-Chinese riots in 1918, along with nearby Mongrave, Pear Tree Grove and Windsor Castle. With regard to animosity against them and their integration into the society, the Chinese of Woodside proper seem to have fared differently from elsewhere. Though the cultivators did "collect",[35] perhaps a euphemism for "steal", the bags of cacao which they had previously sold to him, they offered physical protection from the invading mob to the Chinese grocer. James, the grocer, as the quote below indicates, had been part of the pattern-setting and maintaining agency of the area, the Anglican Church. Emmanual Lord of the Rock Spring Lords, a small family according to the Woodside school registers but one whose name has been in the area since the 1840s, tells the historian Howard Johnson: "James did deh a Woodside, Chinee bway. Him confarm a Woodside church. James, a creole man you haffe call him, and when dem loot Woodside, you see, him haffe run go quite a Rock Spring and go under me auntie bed go hide."[36]

This pot-pourri of people was in constant motion. The school records indicate that on top of the permanent long residents of the area, were several looser groups of persons moving into and out of the village. Children came into the area with adults from Kingston, from other places in St Mary, from the neighbouring parishes of St Ann and St Catherine, from Portland and from faraway Manchester, as well as from Panama. Those moving out left for St Andrew, St Catherine, for college in Kingston and out of the island to British Honduras (now Belize). These registers record the names of guardians as well as the names of children. Many children had surnames different from those of their guardians, an indication that they were either illegitimate children of their guardians or not children of their guardians at all.

The names most often shared by child and guardian are Grant, Stanbury, Walker, Redwood, Williams, Forbes, Hamilton, Anderson, Gillies, Simmonds, Payne, Edwards, Morrison. These data speak of the existence in the area of mother-child units and in some cases, nuclear family structures, but it was not unusual for one of these names to be the guardian of children by another surname, a suggestion here of an extension to the nuclear unit. Apart from the Gillies and the Paynes, all of these names of persons forming mother–child units or nuclear families are known to us from the days of slavery. The structural stability and rootedness of these communities apparently made them attractive places for the wandering to park temporarily, or to park their children temporarily.

The data from the school register also indicate that several families who had lived in the area and made their living here as landowners or tenants in the nineteenth century had a low numerical profile in the church and/or the school in the twentieth century. The Marshalls, Bogles, Bennetts, Conridges and Stewarts, landowners of one to eight acres in 1869–70,[37] had low or no representation among the students registered as attending Woodside School between 1928 and 1948. The same has to be said for the Northovers, Fergusons, Champagnys, Murrays, Huttons, Sheriffes and Ramikis, holders of ten to twenty acres of land in 1882. Some smallholders – the Meades, Lauds/Lords, McKoys, Shaws, Roses and Simmondses among others – also fall in this group.[38] Was it a matter of infertility, few sons to carry on their names, or did parts of these families move out of the area?

The families and individuals involved with the Anglican church and the school were all supported wholly or partially by the land. We have noted that many of those who were baptized into the Anglican faith in the 1850s and 1860s were the children of labourers. Although by the 1880s most of the pre-emancipation sugar and coffee estates in greater Woodside had been abandoned, there was still agriculture-based activity in the area. According to the map of 1880, John Crossman, a name we know from earlier to belong to pre-emancipation land ownership in the area, still held lands close to Smailfield.[39] Here the grandmother of Roy Crossman, a farmer in today's Rock Spring, worked as a labourer, taking her employer's name.[40] Small bits of the slavery-time estates, bought or rented, still grew coffee. William Thomas's Smailfield property, for instance, though it did have fifty-three acres in woods and ruinate, had one acre in coffee; so did Edmund/Edward Marshall's property in Woodside.[41] Help would be needed with the processing of the coffee. Ground provisions were very popular. John Thomas of Smailfield, on the property of I.P. Thomas, had eight acres in ground provisions.[42] He would need help, so would those people with the one acre of cane. In any case, by the end of the nineteenth century, the plantation system was back again in the spaces that had not passed into the hands of the ex-slaves and ex-indentured people and would need labour.

Some pre-emancipation planter families had sold only the outskirts of the plantation, leaving the environs of the great house intact. This was available for sale for the large-scale planting of bananas. Hopewell is a case in point. Most of this property was still intact several years after emancipation and available for the Pringles to establish banana planta-tions thereon. These large scale properties required labour. It was to work on the McNeil estate near Rock Spring that the later set of Morrisons came into the greater Woodside area.[43] Rock Spring now moves from being dominated by the residences of professionals – the doctor, the member of the House of Assembly, the pastor and the stipen-diary magistrate – to being dominated by the residences of middle-class African-Jamaican peasants – Bada Kanali, Bada P. Ramiki – and banana estate workers such as the Morrisons and the Crossmans, who manage to get plots in the early and mid-twentieth century.

The establishment of a banana industry in which there was planting and haulage of the bananas to the wharves created in parts of greater Woodside an economic middle class of ex-slave origin. Woods and ruinate in 1870 had dominated even the very small holdings.[44] Of Conridge's four-acre freehold, one was in ground provisions and the other three in woodland. Of Edward/Edmund Marshall's nine, one was in coffee and eight were in woods and ruinate. Forty-four of the acres in the charge of John Thomas of Smailfield were in woods and ruinate and only eight in ground provisions. Such ruinate could now be put into bananas, either as rented lands or as freeholds.

From the early pre-emancipation days the lands of greater Woodside had grown ground provisions. These fed the enslaved, and to the extent that they could turn their plots into agro-businesses, enhanced the devel-opment of an internal marketing system as well as the diversification of the local agricultural economy. Estates themselves had been into diver-sification as well. One such as Smailfield had, in 1806, plantain walks; plantains, we assume, to be sold for the tables of other whites.[45] It had its pastures where livestock grazed. These were for transportation and for the tables' protein. If we use mixed farming as a measure, we can speak of continuity in the Woodside area between the pre- and the post-emancipation times.

The arrival of banana as an export crop intensified farm activity of all kinds and further encouraged development. More people were at work, too busy in wage employment to keep cows. They needed someone to raise cows and sell them the milk. There was need for more people with carts to take the bananas to the wharves and more people to drive the carts. Old residents such as Levi Hudson talk of the line of banana carts going in convoy over Woodside's hills.[46] There was need for more people to provide mules to draw these carts and more people to grow and cut the grass to feed the mules. There was more need for sugar, thus some like the Grants stayed in sugar, producing raw ("wet") sugar for home consumption and local sales, using their mules to power small iron mills.[47] An adventurous person like "Capry" Brown even tried to move from mule power to water power and turn the old jail in Rock Spring into a sugar factory.[48] Ex-enslaved and ex-indentured workers were thus by the early part of the twentieth century hirers of labour – a significant change.

The economic development of the area, and particularly of Woodside proper, and the change it brought with it, encouraged the authorities to move the post office from the village of Pear Tree Grove, which is in the parish of St Catherine and about three miles away, closer to Woodside proper. According to Mr Vernal Kelly, with whose voice we began this work, the post office was at first in the village called Pear Tree Grove, which is near to Richmond Hill and in the parish of St Catherine.[49] Here there was a great house called "the Works" and apparently sufficient activity to merit such an institution. With the development of the greater Woodside area, it was felt that the post office should be closer, and it was duly moved to Rhyon Hill, which is about a mile from the Woodside School/church. The post office kept its name – Pear Tree Grove P.O. – but the budget was accordingly moved to St Mary.

Rhyon Hill gets its name from the person who owned the piece of land on which the post office stood and who was the postmaster of the shifted post office. Rhyon was an import from St Ann, as we have already mentioned. He owned the house in which the business of the post office was done. Later, the business went to Payne, a friend and neighbour, because according to Mr Kelly, "Rhyon and Payne were . . . fingers, same colour: they were strong together." It was Payne who moved the post office to its present site, another part of St Mary. He ran this business with his daughters, who took over from him in the 1940s.

Neither the name Payne nor the name Rhyon appears on the slave lists, though we do find evidence of Paynes having property in St Mary since 1731 or before.[50] This was Captain Peter Payne, who had one thousand acres close to those of Bathurst, who had four thousand acres in the area between the Knollis and the Flint Rivers. The Paynes and the Rhyons were brown-skinned, curly-haired people. They married with the Browns who had moved into the area in the 1860s. An Adelaide Payne is listed in 1881–82 as controlling five acres of Woodside's lands.[51]

An 1842 reference indicates that the Pear Tree Grove P.O. was in existence then, and was administratively in the parish of St Mary.[52] As we have already mentioned, Miss Jane Collman was one of the earliest of the officers in charge of this institution, whatever its geographic situation. In 1842 this post office served Carron Hall. "Carron Hall, Pear Tree Grove P.O." was the postal address of Reverend Cowan, the representative of the Jamaica Missionary Presbytery; it was also that of the immigration agent, Henry Pupley, who placed it in St Mary.[53] Today the post office remains physically within St Mary but has returned administratively to St Catherine. The mailing address of the citizens of Woodside proper is Woodside, Pear Tree Grove P.O., St Catherine. This post office continues to be used by most of the citizens of greater Woodside whose residences are still administratively in St Mary.

Poor Pear Tree Grove — or was it "rich" Pear Tree Grove? For it was perhaps the attractive sound of its name that made so many choose it for their property — now here, now there, physically and administratively. If we look at the detail of the 1952 map in map 8, we see two Pear Tree Groves in relatively close proximity. On the 1880 map (map 4), Pear Tree Grove, said to be "formerly Spring Valley", is on the east rather than the south-west, as it is on the 1952 map. The Pear Tree Grove close to Woodside on the 1952 map is the point to which the post office was moved in the early decade of the twentieth century. The switches and movements of the name "Pear Tree Grove" are mirrored in the demographic history of the area in the early years of that century.

Let us look once more at the school. If we go by the fluctuation in the numbers of children admitted or readmitted to the Woodside School, we see that the development of the area was attended by continued movement of people to and from the area. In 1928 there had been sixty-two admissions. The number rose in the following year to seventy-six, a jump of fourteen. It was much the same in 1930, being seventy-

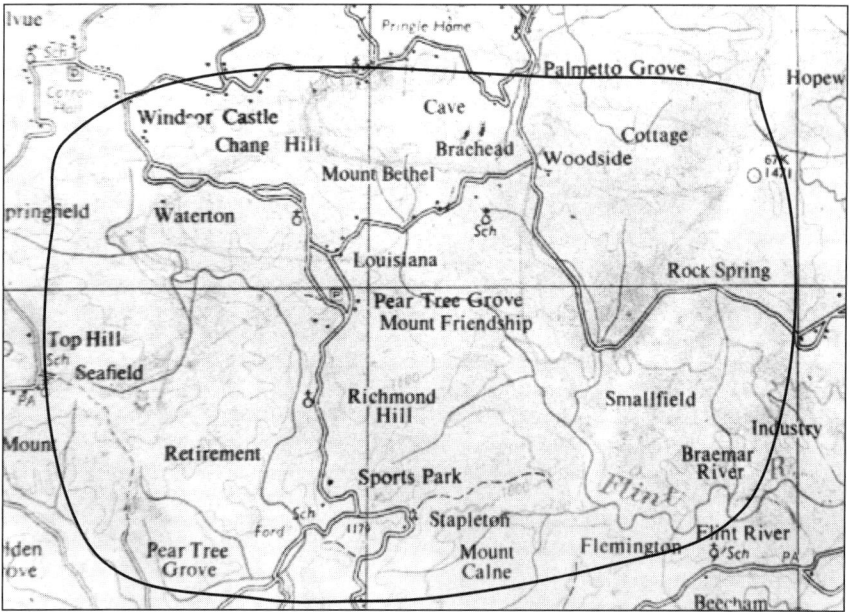

Map 8 Detail of a 1952 survey map showing two Pear Tree Groves (photo by Martin Mordecai)

eight. By 1931 it had fallen by twenty, to fifty-eight. It increased by five in the next year, to sixty-three, decreased by three to sixty in 1933, and was up again by eight in 1934, to sixty-eight. It fell again in 1935 by seven, to sixty-one, and in 1936 was at the all-time low of forty-nine. In 1937 it rose by nine to fifty-eight, and again by nine in 1938, to sixty-seven. The admissions were at their highest in 1939, at eighty-eight, having jumped by twenty-one. It levelled off to eighty-four in 1940, but by 1941 it was seventy-seven. The year after, it was up again to eighty-six, and in 1943 and 1944 it was fifty-seven. It sank to fifty-one in 1945, moved up to sixty-five in 1946, sank again in 1947 to fifty-one, and was sixty-one in 1947.

These fluctuations cannot be correlated with acts of God such as the hurricanes of 1933 and 1944, or with such political events as the general riots of 1938 and universal adult suffrage in 1944. The data for school attendance are not as those for admission, annual, and are therefore of limited comparative value. They tell us, if we can take them seriously, that day school attendance was very stable, being on average 136 for 1911, one less in 1925, and also 135 in 1941. The school, according to these data, continued to serve a stable social base of students with

others floating in and out, and no doubt in and out of the nuclear families to which they were attached temporarily.

Children moving out to high school contributed to the sense of a floating population. The education given by Woodside School was of good
quality, measured by standards set in Jamaica. In 1935 one of the family of late-arriving Walkers won the parish scholarship for children ten
to twelve years old. This scholarship acknowledged him to be the most
academically gifted child in the parish and gave him a place in a school
in Kingston, the island's capital, which is forty miles away. The acco-
lade went in the following year to a girl, one of the later Williamses,
with the same consequence. Other children were selected for high school
by virtue of their success at entrance examinations. They too moved
out of Woodside and went to Kingston. Other children stayed in the
village and, after completing their elementary education at Woodside
School, sat and passed the national examinations — the Jamaica Local
Examinations. This qualified them for entry into colleges preparing lower
professionals such as teachers and sanitary inspectors. Several of
Woodside's young floated out of the village in this way between 1928
and 1948, to distinguish themselves nationally and internationally.

William John Neilson had, like these twentieth-century Woodside children, left the area in 1801 at about aged ten for a life outside of
Woodside and outside of Jamaica.[54] William John returned by 1811,
trained in physic and surgery and to live, to farm and no doubt to practise his craft in the greater Woodside area.[55] The other professionals we
met in greater Woodside in the days of slavery must have done likewise
for there was little scope for professional training in the island then,
and none in Woodside. The Walker and Williams children of the mid-
twentieth century left and likewise were trained in the professions; they,
however, did not return. The twentieth-century world in which they
found their places excluded Woodside from their network of connections, whereas William John Neilson's Woodside had a clearly, established place within the wider nineteenth-century world. He and it were
part of a set of agro-businesses linked into a system which recognized
them throughout the international world of commerce. His Woodside
was an economic unit linked in an immediate sense with this larger world
through his sale of coffee to Kingston, to Britain and his shipment of a
house from Woodside to St Elizabeth, more than a hundred miles away.

The peasants of twentieth-century Woodside and their children had no such economic circumstance from which to derive a national or international identity. They were isolates in the larger world of economics and finance. John Neilson had passed on his Woodside estate to his son William John, who had passed it on to his son George and, should he predecease him, to his younger son William John.[56] William John, the father, had dispensed his fortune in this way though he had four daughters, all older than his sons. Clearly the British system of entail was at work here. Passing on one's estate intact usually creates a gentry which, wittingly or not, assumes a pattern-setting and maintaining function in the village of which it is a part, supporting the church in its moral and ideological stance.

Even if the Neilson sons were minded to play the gentry with its sociological associations, the family's psychological and economic collapse made this impossible. A similar tale could no doubt be recited for the other "master" families in greater Woodside. The Neilsons gave their great house and their share of the pattern-setting and maintaining role to the Anglican Church, but the church did not fully replace the estate for the church/school combine did not make itself into an economic and social unit to replace the estate as the link between the village and the wider national and international world.[57] Reconnection with such a Woodside could neither provide young professionals with the opportunity to practise skills learned on the outside, nor give them the sense of connectedness to the wider world that their cultivated minds now needed. They would have to create these links. Did the church/school give them the confidence to do so?

The church/school, the major institution in the public domain in twentieth-century Woodside, rather than being an economic entity like Neilson's plantation had been, was a value-orienting institution. Associated with this was an external emphasis. Such conditions helped to make the greater Woodside area of the early twentieth century into a dormitory from which its academically bright minds graduated to a place with which Woodside had no immediate and firmly established institutional links. For these brighter African-Jamaican minds to return Woodside to its place in the national and international world was a difficult task. They left Woodside with its "manyness", Woodside, an embedded rock collage over which waves continually ebb and flow, the flow outwards destined to dominate, to fracture the variegated rock into pieces and to sweep these pieces into other lands.

Afterword

Sociological Perspectives

By the beginning of the twentieth century new kinds of people had merged in greater Woodside. There was the great African-Jamaican majority, no longer slaves; there were people from India, new to the behaviour of the African Jamaicans with whom they now lived and worked; and there were Chinese, also new to the African Jamaicans. Though it had been the intention of those who ultimately controlled this area and the rest of Jamaica to make of the African Jamaicans a caste of labourers, no one had explicitly told them so, with the result that they assumed themselves to be in charge of their possibilities and destiny, and where it was at all possible tried to make themselves into landholding small farmers. There was a significant measure of success in this regard in the greater Woodside area. It was a success too for the Indians who had been recruited as indentured labour. Surrounding these "ought-to-have-been-labourers" and former indentured workers, were a few plantation-style businesses controlled by whites, new to the area, by black and brown professionals, also new to the area, and by clerics, usually white and foreign. This mix was itself new. New ways of doing the things necessary for maintaining personal life and social life could possibly ensue out of this new equation. The area could see new institutions.

Under slavery masters had been the principal source of the African Jamaicans' supply of animal protein and clothing, and though enslaved persons did cultivate their own plots, these were the property of their masters and in many cases ceased to be available after emancipation. We have seen that by purchase as well as other forms of obtaining lands, the African-Jamaican population took over the task of providing for itself; we have seen how it fed itself after slavery and produced surpluses to be sold to others. Here again was a new kind of behaviour. This new behaviour encouraged other new behaviour. It created new forms of livelihood such as produce-dealing, in which the Chinese, among others, participated. With their involvement in agriculture, African Jamaicans continued on a smaller scale the coffee and sugar planting and production that the white planters in the area had begun. The Indians in the area took part in these agricultural activities as well. African Jamaicans, Indo- and Sino-Jamaicans had, with this move, stepped out of their forebears' service roles and into self-employment; not all of them, of course, but enough of them to change the perception others had of them and to change their perceptions of themselves.

African Jamaicans had tried to fill the gaps in the distribution of imported goods created by the exit of the slavery system. Their need for these goods was increasingly more than their ability to supply them. This condition produced opportunities for the Chinese and Lebanese, who entered this field as well, to do a better job and to carve out a niche in the economy for themselves. We have noted in the last chapter, the presence in Woodside in 1918 of the Chinese shopkeeper, James, and of the Lebanese name, Khouri, associated with lands on which the Baptists had built their church. Woodside clearly made a place for the special skills of the people from the Far and Middle East.

The white planters in the slavery days had seen to the management of public issues through the parish Vestry and the House of Assembly. Participation in these agencies required a particular economic status. The planter class in greater Woodside continued to be involved in the politics of the country. The evidence at hand shows only one African Jamaican to have been an elector in the early post-emancipation period.[1] The political system was changed after 1866. Now the Colonial Office in Britain assumed the function of a representative government and governed through a resident governor. Petitioning of the rulers had been a popular option for people who did not have the franchise. It remained so after 1866. Limited representation returned at the beginning of the twentieth century but the franchise remained out of the reach of all but a few of Woodside's peasants. The petition to the Queen through her representative, the governor of Jamaica, remained the people's route to political ventilation.

Figure 4 Woodside deputation at Headquarters House, petitioning the government (*Daily Gleaner*, 7 February 1941)

Chinese Jamaicans shared with African Jamaicans this mode of and apparent faith in the efficacy of the petition, as is evidenced from the photograph above (see figure 4). In this 1941 photograph, there are seven petitioners to the Honourable F.L. Brown, acting colonial secretary. They are all male. In the group are the area's elected parish representatives at the national and local government levels. The other four members of the group petitioning on behalf of north-western St Mary, the greater Woodside area, are ordinary citizens. They all reside in Woodside. One is the Chinese grocer, Willy Lee Lim, who is a recent import into the area; one is Ernest Brodber, resident in the area for just a year; one is M.A. Rennalls, the headmaster of Woodside School and an import; and the other is Vernal Kelly, the last named already known to readers. Note that of those waiting on the acting colonial secretary on behalf of their area, only Vernal Kelly has an ancestral history in the area that goes back to slavery: a forebear of his had been a slave on Woodside proper's estate between 1817 and 1834.[2] The new people coming into Woodside were apparently allowed by the great black majority, there from the days of slavery, to make links on their behalf with the political authorities outside.

Obviously the people of Woodside were, before 1944 and universal suffrage, minor actors in the arrangements established for ruling the country of which they were a part. In the heyday of the slave master, the Vestry, the parish political organization, had assumed many functions of governance of Woodside. As we have seen, the greater Woodside area was well stocked with Vestrymen. It had also had its resident members of the House of Assembly. By the mid-twentieth century, the Vestry's significance within the Jamaican political system had diminished and most of its governing functions switched to the central government. This move took potential power out of the village. Political significance for early black twentieth-century Woodside would now have to be measured in terms of visibility at the national political and administrative level. Black Woodside's only connection at this level, before 1944, was the job of the waywarden. These people had the task of seeing to the state of small lengths of the highway in their area. Hugh Walker and Thomas Walsh had these responsibilities in greater Woodside, the former for part of the Woodside road, the latter for part of the Palmetto Grove road.[3] Both of these, according to oral reports, were African-Jamaicans.

The arrangements for religious worship in Woodside mirrored Woodside's involvement with politics and public administration before 1944 and the coming of universal suffrage. External control is common to both. The Anglican Church, the Baptist Church, the Presbyterian Church, the Salvation Army and the Seventh-Day Adventist Church, the last two coming into the area later than the others, were not arrangements which Woodside people devised; they were arrangements into which they were usually invited, without their even having to petition for inclusion. There were, however, ways of praising their God which they devised. Martha Beckwith records, and oral sources confirm, the existence of Convince cults in the Hopewell area.[4] This is a form of worship in which links are made with the spirit of the ancestors. Oral sources also tell of a spot in the Rock Spring–John Crow Spring area which had been and still remains consecrated to African-Jamaican religious rites.[5]

It was also customary for individuals to feel themselves touched by their God, to feel that He had sent them personally on warning and teaching missions, and to accept the charge to do so.

It is the middle-class professionals with their connections to the wider world that give social legitimacy to behaviour. The local religious creations, usually a mix of bits and pieces remembered from Africa, knotted into strands from the foreign churches, did not have their help; the local creations thus had to remain at grass-roots level without the literary and conceptual skills of the socially mobile. Some of these religious re-creations doubled as occasions of and for recreation. *Manalva* already discussed, is one such. Celebrations of this African-derived occasion went late into the night, spectators being charged a fee and foodstuff being on sale. Such forms, whether religious or secular recreation, were class coded. *Manalva* and other Afro-oriented behaviour belonged to those not geared for upward social mobility. More middle-class forms of recreation were cantatas and eisteddfods, which like the formal religious worship, were the brain-children of the public pattern-setters, the church/school. Middle class these forms may have been, but they were, like the Afro-oriented forms, open to all. Woodside's people chose as they saw fit. We have seen in the last chapter how they chose to disaggregate the church/school system and take what they wished from it – instruction for their children.

Beneath these institutional activities – education, recreation, the worshipping of one's God, participation in the wider polity and the satisfying of the need for food and clothes – lay a web of kinship relations that generally excluded the teachers, the clergy, the Chinese grocer and the most recent migrants. A foundation myth comments on the attitude of the people of Woodside proper towards kinship.[6] It claims that the area began with some male ex-slaves – Ferguson, Forbes, Hermit, Marshall, Lemorsely, Walker – to whom Mrs Neilson sold her property. All had children with the same woman, named, appropriately, Granny Cous[in]. Their offspring intermarried. All the surnames appear on the tax roll of 1869–80 as users of land formerly Woodside. All these names, except for Ferguson, Marshall and Lemorsely, appear on the baptismal list of the Anglican church for the period 1817–34; and Ferguson and Marshall are indeed on the slave returns of Dr Neilson for the years 1817 and 1820, along with the others, except Hermitt. Since these people were around since slavery (with the exception of Lemorsely, which appears on none of the lists I have seen), the founding must, in the village mind, be dated from the time when ex-slaves became proprietors.

It is a fact, as the slave returns for Woodside proper show, that Mary Ann Drew did mother men with the names of some of those above. This African-born lady, nineteen years old at the birth of Edward John Marshall in 1813, twenty-three at the birth of Billy Ferguson, and thirty-one and thirty-three years old at the birth of her children by Forbes, had many more child-bearing years in which to produce by Hermitt and Lemorsely, and this around the time of emancipation in 1838. Could she have been Granny Cous? Our data do not allow us to comment on this. We do know, though, that Fergusons, Forbeses, Hermits, and Walkers did intermarry and inter-mate after emancipation, and that two brothers in this group produced children by two sisters, and that another set of brothers mated with a woman and her niece.

More important than whether there is truth to this myth, is the fact that it exists. The myth's existence points to a feeling within the village of an "us", the founding families versus "them", the new arrivals. It also points to a preference for endogamy. We have seen, along with the above mentioned family connections, the Hudson-Fyffe connection of Rock Spring, and a connection between these and the later arriving Walkers, who themselves married into the Forbes clan, whom we know have connections with Fergusons and with Hermitts. We know too that Bolts married Conridge, and that Wrights married into the Hamilton clan, as well as into the Grant clan, which was itself connected to the Browns. We have already noted the kinship spread of these latter families, and there are many other internal marriage and mating connections.

This endogamous trend towards marriage and mating appears to be new. It was not the way in pre-emancipation Woodside among the white population. Mates had come from within the area but they had come as well from Kingston and from England. Of course with movement of the African-Jamaican population proscribed, endogamy was mandated. That this system continued after slavery and into the twentieth century, when geographic mobility was possible, suggests that it was the preferred style of the African Jamaican. It ought to have led to stability; it could on the other hand, stultify.

Another difference between the Woodside of freedom and the Woodside of enslavement exists in the relative place of the woman. While

Mrs Neilson, Mrs Turner and Mrs Burrowes, among others, were owners of property and in the case of Mrs Neilson and Mrs Burrowes at
some time, the directors of their own agro-businesses, the black woman,
as we have mentioned above, seems to be less involved with the ownership of property. Why would one who had cultivated her own farm, and
had, as women usually did in slavery, carried the brunt of field work,
not be among the new owners? Holt mentions the frequency with which
women were involved in fracas with overseers about the rights to time.[7]
One of the things they apparently wanted time to do, was to see to the
care of their children. With no old woman designated by an estate to
see to the care of the children, and no ability to hire nannies as Mrs
Neilson and Burrowes could do, child care after emancipation fell to
natural mothers who probably preferred this to any other job. There
was less time to earn the money with which to buy land. With no land
to inherit, to be supported became an attractive alternative, and economic dependency on men became a social fact. With his name now officially given to his children, with land and with a woman dependent on
him, the Woodside man was set to become the self-directed patriarch he
had not been in slavery. The child-caring option discouraged geographic
mobility. So did farming. If Woodside's women did take the child-
caring option, then the village was on the way to being one in which
the economic power lay with the men.

It is in the area of African-related recreation that we get the strongest
impression of black women. Cousin Miss, the granddaughter of Bada
Kanali, renamed Hudson by his masters, was the Queen in the *Manalva*
celebrations. Her memory is only eclipsed by that of Mrs Jane Eliza
Neilson, whom one resident likens to the white witch of Rose Hall.[8] It
is the black women, these embedded rocks in control of the homes,
who passed on an African-influenced cuisine – pounding plantains into
a foo-foo, for instance. It was they who tried to maintain endogamy by
making the life of "foreign wives" difficult and institutionalizing a "born
ya" versus a "just-me-come" dichotomy into village thinking and
action.[9]

We have seen Mr Kelly's comment that Rhyon and Payne were both
of the same colour and were "fingers" and therefore passed the job of
postmaster from one to the other. There is not enough data to make
any more comment on colour as a factor in Woodside's sociology;
suffice it to say that there tended to be areas in which brown-skinned

people lived. Aitkin Town was one such. It was and is physically part
of Woodside proper and had fallen into the hands of the Aitkins, the
Browns (Indians), the Paynes and the Colemans, who inter-mated to produce brown-skinned, curly-haired offspring. Aitkin Town continued to
bear this distinction well into the mid- and late-twentieth century, but
neither the economic status of the brown-skinned people of Aitkin Town,
however, nor their educational status, carry any suspicion of an elite. It
is instead tempting to propose that there was a black-skinned elite, which
was Anglican and was going off to high school. The teachers in the elementary school, from all reports, tended also to be of obvious African
ancestry, so that educational achievement tended to be seen to have a
black skin. This "elite" galvanized the traditional families of whatever
colour, and the newcomers as well as the Indians and coloureds, around
Anglican values, each of these sectors being able to return to their central values as was necessary.

The tendency towards endogamy just described could have engen-
dered social stability within the area. A division of sex roles, such that
men have property and women are economically dependent on them,
could have made this social stability one in which social power was in
male hands. But for a stable patriarchal society to emerge, Woodside's
men would have to know themselves to be and be seen to be a unit, one
which controlled the area's interaction with the wider and public world.
None of these circumstances existed, though given the patriarchal nature
of the churches, those offices would pass exclusively to them. But here
these men's interests were subordinated to that of the church, and this
community of Christians further divided them into discrete denominations. No really conscious grouping of males can be said to have emerged
in the greater Woodside area or in Woodside proper by which men
were linked exclusively to a wider and public society. The linkage
between the village and the outside world was the business of the
church/school rather than that of landholding men. In addition, the most
visible part of the church/school system, the elementary school, had in
the existence of the assistant teachers, more female authority figures than
male.

That public power in the village was located outside of it and outside
of their families was a fact which the several children socialized by the
church/school could not fail to internalize. They knew that their own
search for power would also have to be located outside. It is to this out-

side that they went for secondary education. The social function of education is to provide an area with its creators. Training outside of the physical environment in which students are to apply their creative energies tends to teach them how to relate to that outside environment rather than to the home base, so that even when students from rural Woodside were trained in agriculture, their newly acquired skills could not be available to, and were not applicable to, Woodside. For one thing, they were trained to serve rather than to create and this in branches of the civil service, no outposts of which were in the greater Woodside area. Thus, not even the presence of those should-be role models was available to the socialization process. Mr Vernal Kelly, who had a passion for agriculture, did not return to reside and farm in the area until he had reached the age of retirement.

Such a pattern of education inhibited the development of a residential African-Chinese-Indian-Lebanese creative middle class, for all ethnic groups shared the value placed on the church/school. The association that we see here between non-residence and creativity is quite different from the situation which existed in the greater Woodside of the early nineteenth century, where a clergyman of the established and prestigious Anglican church lived and reared his family, where a surgeon, lawyers, financiers, a member of the House of Assembly and stipendiary magistrates lived close by. The possibility of migration to Cuba in the early decades of the twentieth century, which many Jamaicans, including Ernest Brown from Woodside, took, and later of short term migration as contract labour to British Honduras and the United States, as Roland Forbes did, furthered the orientation to the outside and the depletion of the pool of residential creative energy.[10] This was Woodside at the time of universal suffrage and the years immediately after — an area set to and continuing to lose its potential creators.

Notes

Chapter 1

1. StM 1208, Map Collection, National Library of Jamaica, Kingston. All other maps mentioned in this chapter are found at the National Library of Jamaica.
2. StM 1436.
3. StM 946.
4. StM 1226.
5. StM 1244.
6. Deeds LOS 687, 164, Island Records Office, Twickenham Park, Jamaica. All other deeds mentioned in this chapter are found in this office.
7. Deeds LOS 487, 109.
8. Deeds LOS 489, 169.
9. StM 1089.
10. Deeds LOS 487, 109.
11. StM 583.
12. StM 569.
13. StM 601.
14. StM 156.
15. B.W. Higman, *Jamaica Surveyed* (Kingston: Institute of Jamaica Publications, 1988), 204, 264, 265.
16. Ibid., 203.
17. Phillip Wright, *Lady Nugent's Journal of Her Residence in Jamaica from 1801 to 1805* (Kingston: University of the West Indies Press, 2002), 300.
18. StM 583.
19. Great Britain Parliament, House of Commons, Select Committee on Sugar and Coffee Planting (1848), 229.
20. StM 144.

Chapter 2

1. *Jamaica Almanack,* 1811.
2. Wills 109, folio nos. 112 and 110, folio 103, Island Records Office, Twickenham Park, Jamaica. All other wills and all deeds mentioned in this chapter are found in this office.
3. Deeds 687, folio no. 164.
4. StM 569, Map Collection, Institute of Jamaica, Kingston.
5. *Jamaica Almanack,* 1821.
6. *Jamaica Almanack,* 1826.
7. See Register of Slave Returns (St Mary) 1B/11/7/92, signed by William John Neilson, at the Jamaica Archives, Spanish Town.
8. Wills 109, folio nos. 112 and 110, folio no. 103.
9. *Jamaica Almanack,* 1826.
10. Crop accounts 1B/11/4/ folio no. 70.43, Jamaica Archives. All other crop accounts mentioned in this chapter are found at the Jamaica Archives.
11. See Register of Slave Returns 1929, 1B/11/7/113, filed under the name of estate of William John Neilson, Jamaica Archives.
12. Deeds LOS 75.4.
13. *Jamaica Almanack,* 1832.
14. Ibid.
15. Appendix to the seventh report from the Select Committee on Sugar and Coffee Planting, Parliament of Great Britain, House of Commons (1848), 229.
16. Crop accounts 1B/11/4/77/230.
17. Crop accounts 1B/11/4, folio no. 88.2.
18. Crop accounts 1B/11/4/70/43.
19. Crop accounts 1B/11/4/81/24.
20. *Jamaica Almanack,* 1811.
21. Deeds 687, folio no. 164.
22. *Jamaica Almanack,* 1821.
23. Ibid., 1826.
24. Ibid., 1828.
25. Ibid., 1832.
26. Ibid., 1840.
27. StM 1436, Map Collection, National Library of Jamaica, Kingston. Another undated map, StM 1244, appears to describe the disputed land. This map mentions Burrowes's land as a boundary. All other maps mentioned in this chapter are found at the National Library.
28. Discussions with Mr Arnold Remikie and other Rock Spring residents, 1993.
29. *Jamaica Almanack,* 1840.

30. Ibid., 1821, 1826, 1828, 1832.
31. Ibid., 1832.
32. Crop accounts 1B/11/4/81.24.
33. StM 136.
34. See map in the introduction.
35. *Jamaica Almanack,* 1826.
36. Ibid., 1828, 1832.
37. Ibid., 1840.
38. Appendix to the seventh report from the Select Committee on Sugar and Coffee Planting, Parliament of Great Britain, House of Commons (1848), 229.
39. Crop accounts 1B/11/3/83/174.
40. *Jamaica Almanack,* 1828, 1832.
41. Ibid., 1821.
42. Ibid., 1840.
43. Ibid., 1826.
44. Contributed by Bishie Walker at a lecture at the first George Beckford Memorial at Woodside, St Mary, 1991.
45. *Jamaica Almanack,* 1821, 1826, 1832.
46. Crop accounts 1B/11/4/73/27.
47. Crop accounts 1B/11/4/78/219.
48. Crop accounts 1B/11/4/83/223.
49. Crop accounts 1B/11/4/82/144.
50. StM 1226.
51. *Jamaica Almanack,* 1821.
52. Ibid., 1826.
53. Ibid., 1828.
54. Ibid., 1840.
55. Appendix to the seventh report from the Select Committee on Sugar and Coffee Planting, Parliament of Great Britain, House of Commons (1848), 229.
56. Crop accounts 1B/11/11/81/15.
57. *Jamaica Almanack,* 1824.
58. Crop accounts 1B/11/4/83/221.
59. Appendix to the seventh report from the Select Committee on Sugar and Coffee Planting, Parliament of Great Britain, House of Commons (1848), 229.
60. Ibid.
61. *Jamaica Almanack,* 1811.
62. Ibid., 1821.
63. Ibid., 1824.
64. Ibid., 1828.

65. StM 1109.
66. *Jamaica Almanack,* 1824.
67. Ibid., 1826.
68. StM 51.
69. Register of Baptisms 1817–1829, Marriages 1817–1825 and 1828, Burials 1817–1825 (St Mary), vol. 2, Jamaica Archives.
70. Deeds LOS 687, folio no. 164.
71. *Jamaica Almanack,* 1840.
72. See Register of Slave Returns (St Mary) 1829, filed under McCrae 1B/11/7/113, Jamaica Archives.
73. Crop accounts 1B/11/4/78/219.
74. Deeds 687, 164.
75. StM 572.
76. StM 139.
77. StM 94.
78. StM 708.
79. *Baptist Missionary Herald,* February 1831, 14. Collection of the Baptist Church, Kingston, Jamaica.
80. *Jamaica Almanack,* 1811, 24.
81. Ibid., 1840.
82. Baptism Register for Slaves (St Mary), Jamaica Archives.
83. Wright, *Lady Nugent's Journal,* 77–78.
84. Ibid.
85. *Jamaica Almanack,* 1811, 1821, 1824, 1826, 1828, 1832, 1840 for the rest of the paragraph.

Chapter 3

1. Deeds LOS 269, folio no. 181, Island Records Office, Twickenham Park, Jamaica. All other deeds and all wills mentioned in this chapter are found in this office.
2. Deeds LOS 333, folio no. 188.
3. Deeds LOS 48, 195.
4. Deeds LOS 487, folio no. 169.
5. Deeds LOS 487, folio no. 109.
6. Wright, *Lady Nugent's Journal,* 206–7.
7. Register of Baptisms 1817–1829, Marriages 1817–1825 and 1828, Burials 1817–1825 (St Mary), vol. 2, Jamaica Archives. All other references in this chapter to registers of baptism, marriage, births and deaths are also from this source.
8. Ibid.

9. Deeds LOS 786, folio no. 167.

10. *Jamaica Almanack, 1811–1827.*

11. StM 946, Map Collection, National Library of Jamaica, Kingston. All other maps mentioned in this chapter are found at the National Library of Jamaica.

12. Register of Baptisms 1817–1829, Marriages 1817–1825 and 1828, Burials 1817–1825 (St Mary), vol. 2.

13. See R.L. Williams, *The Coffee Industry of Jamaica* (Kingston: Institute of Social and Economic Research, University of the West Indies, 1975), 2.

14. Wright, *Lady Nugent's Journal,* 243.

15. Deeds LOS 687, folio no. 164.

16. Edward Brathwaite, *The Development of Creole Society in Jamaica 1770–1820* (Oxford: Clarendon Press, 1971), chapter 3.

17. Register of Baptisms 1817–1829, Marriages 1817–1825 and 1828, Burials 1817–1825 (St Mary), vol. 2.

18. Ibid., 1826–1857.

19. See Register of Baptisms 1817–1829, Marriages 1817–1825 and 1828, Burials 1817–1825 (St Mary), vol. 2. Also CO 137/261 Metcalfe to Stanley 1842 encl. Report from the C'ttee to whom was referred the petition of the freeholder and inhabitants of the western part of the parish of St George and the eastern part of St Mary, Jamaica Archives.

20. Evidence of John Fyffe. There is a Fyffe House on the map of 1880. See also the above.

21. See Douglas Hall, *Free Jamaica* (New Haven: Yale University Press, 1959), for several references to Fyfe/Fyffe.

22. Deeds LOS 487, folio no. 109.

23. Deeds LOS 589, folio no. 186.

24. Wills 110, folio nos. 103 and 109, folio no. 112.

25. Deeds LOS 786, folio no. 167.

26. Register of Baptisms 1817–1829, Marriages 1817–1825 and 1828, Burials 1817–1825 (St Mary), vol. 2.

27. Crop accounts 1B/11/4/70/43, Jamaica Archives. All other crop accounts mentioned in this chapter are found in these archives.

28. Wills 110, folio no. 103.

29. Register of Slave Returns (St Mary) 1929, filed under Neilson 1B/11/7/113, Jamaica Archives.

30. *Baptist Missionary Herald*, February 1835. Collection of the Baptist Church, Kingston, Jamaica.

31. See epitaph in the introduction and map of Smailfield in chapter 1.

32. Register of Slave Returns (St Mary) 1820, filed under Burrowes 1B/11/7/42, Jamaica Archives.

33. Crop accounts 1B/11/4/81/15.
34. See Wills 110, folio no. 103.
35. Lucille Mathurin, "A Historical Study of Women in Jamaica from 1655–1844" (PhD diss., University of the West Indies, Mona, Jamaica, 1974).
36. Throughout this work, Lady Nugent notes the absence of white women. At Hopewell she sees mulattos – "daughters of members of the assembly of officers etc. etc." (78).
37. StM 1089.
38. See Wills 110, folio no. 103.
39. Register of Baptisms 1817–1829, Marriages 1817–1825 and 1828, Burials 1817–1825 (St Mary), vols. 2 and 4.
40. Deeds LOS 589, folio no. 186
41. Ibid.
42. Deeds LOS 503, folio no. 45; LOS 521, folio no. 3.
43. Deeds LOS 687, folio no. 164.
44. Deeds LOS 487, folio no. 109.
45. Deeds LOS 589, folio no. 186.
46. *Jamaica Almanack,* 1811–1840.
47. Ibid.

Chapter 4

1. Wright, *Lady Nugent's Journal,* 318.
2. Swithin Wilmot, "St Mary/Woodside Area: General History Sketches" (paper presented at a series of lectures in Woodside, 4 January 1995).
3. Register of Baptisms 1826–1857 (St Mary), vol. 4, Jamaica Archives, Spanish Town.
4. Register of Baptisms, Marriages and Burials, 1817–1829 (St Mary and St Thomas-ye-Vale), vol. 2, Jamaica Archives.
5. Igor Kopytoff and Suzanne Miers, *Slavery in Africa* (Madison: University of Wisconsin Press, 1977), 40.
6. Wright, *Lady Nugent's Journal,* 77–78.
7. Ibid., 235.
8. Crop accounts 16/11/4/67/102, Jamaica Archives. All other crop accounts mentioned in this chapter are found in these archives.
9. Register of Slave Returns (St Mary) 1B/11/7/5, 6, 42, 54, 92, Jamaica Archives.
10. She observes of the Sherriff establishment, "The house is perfectly in Creole style. A number of Negroes, men, women and children, running and lying

about, in all parts of it. Never in my life did I smell so many." Wright, *Lady Nugent's Journal*, 76.

11. Ibid., 78.

12. Ibid.

13. Ibid., 72.

14. Brathwaite, *The Development of Creole Society*, 165.

15. Higman, *Jamaica Surveyed*, 270–271, and Register of Slave Returns (St Mary) 1B/11/7/5,6&42, Jamaica Archives.

16. Register of Slave Returns IB/11/7/5, 6, 42, 54, Jamaica Archives.

17. "With Forebears from Guinea" (48StcFa), 6, parish of St Catherine, in Erna Brodber, "Life in Jamaica in the Early Twentieth Century: A Presentation of Ninety Oral Accounts" (typescript, Institute of Social and Economic Research Documentation Centre, University of the West Indies, Jamaica, 1980).

18. Higman, *Jamaica Surveyed*, 293–97.

19. Wright, *Lady Nugent's Journal*, 29, and Orlando Patterson, *Sociology of Slavery* (Kingston: Sangster's Book Stores, 1967), chapters 1 and 6.

20. Gad Heuman, *Between Black and White* (Westport: Greenwood Press, 1981), 5.

21. See list of slaves from Petersfield and note from map of 1804 that there were property owners called Forbes in the areas mentioned. See also Hopewell list for Redwood, and note from Wright (*Lady Nugent's Journal*, 313) that Redwood had holdings in nearby St Catherine. Also see Brathwaite's appendix to *The Development of Creole Society*, for news of Redwood as magistrate for St Mary in 1787.

22. Laura Lomas, interview with Mr John Fyffe of Rock Spring, 24 July 1993. Also personal communications with Mr Fyffe.

23. See reference in F.G. Cassidy and R.B. Le Page, eds., *Dictionary of Jamaican English*, 2nd ed. (Kingston: University of the West Indies Press, 2002).

24. See list of slaves for Brae Head in preceding pages.

25. *Jamaica Almanack*, 1840.

26. See Register of Baptisms 1826–1857 (St Mary), vol. 4, Jamaica Archives, Spanish Town and Register of Baptisms, Marriages and Burials, 1817–1829 (St Mary and St Thomas-ye-Vale), vol. 2, Jamaica Archives.

27. Crop accounts 1B/11/4/73/227.

28. Crop accounts 1B/11/4/70/43.

29. See "Oral Historian" (StjFa), 5–6, parish of St James, in Brodber, "Life in Jamaica".

30. Brathwaite, *Development of Creole Society*, 159.

31. *Jamaica Almanack*, 1832.

32. Crop accounts 1B/11/4/81/24.

33. *Jamaica Almanack,* 1811.
34. Ibid., 1826.
35. Ibid., 1821.
36. Deeds LOS 487, folio no. 169, Jamaica Archives.
37. *Jamaica Almanack,* 1824.
38. Ibid., 1821.
39. See Register of Baptisms 1826–1857 (St Mary), vol. 4, Jamaica Archives, Spanish Town.
40. *Baptist Missionary Herald,* March 1838. Collection of the Baptist Church, Kingston, Jamaica.
41. Wills 109, folio nos. 112 and 110, folio no. 103, Island Records Office, Twickenham Park, Jamaica.
42. Proceedings of the House of Assembly of Jamaica, Kingston, 1826.

Chapter 5

1. Jamaica Minutes of the Council, July 1932–September 1839, 1B/5/3/24, Jamaica Archives, Spanish Town.
2. *Handbook of Jamaica,* 1901.
3. CO 137/210, Special Magistrate's Report no. 10, 1/3/1836, Sligo to Glenelg. Microfilm, West Indies Collection, University of the West Indies, Mona, Jamaica.
4. CO 137/209–343 (1835–59), Special Magistrates' Reports. Microfilm, West Indies Collection, University of the West Indies, Mona, Jamaica.
5. Hall, *Free Jamaica,* 110fn.
6. This and other references to the testimony of John Fyffe of Rock Spring come from Lomas, interview with John Fyffe, as well as his personal communications with the author.
7. Hall, *Free Jamaica,* 110 (fn).
8. According to the Register of Baptisms (St Mary) 1826–1857, Jamaica Archives, a Letitia Lindsay was baptized in Rock Spring 26 December 1854 – evidence that there were some adult Lindsays and that they were likely to have been around when Fyfe was an official in the area.
9. Dr Swithin Wilmot of the Department of History, University of the West Indies, Mona, in private communications, advises me that Captain Alexander Gordon Fyfe had helped to quell the rebellion in the west of the island in 1831 known as the Sam Sharpe Rebellion, and that he had led the Maroons in 1865 in the quelling of that uprising called the Morant Bay Rebellion. Fyfe is also the subject of documented comments from the governor to the Colonial Office. In 1836 his stipendiary report is called by the governor, in

his dispatch to the colonial secretary, "a sensible one". See CO 137/212, dispatch 401, Sligo to Glenelg. In 1859 the governor writes to the Colonial Office concerning Fyfe: "The residence of Mr Fyfe is at present in Portland of which parish he was appointed custos . . . by governor Sir Henry Barkly with a view to restoring its affairs which both socially and financially were lamentably disordered." Fyfe did a very good job, effected, the missive continues, by Fyfe's "personal influence" and "judicious exercise of authority". Fyfe had his many other duties but the governor was suggesting that more special magistrates be put under him, that Walsh, the former stipendiary magistrate now living in St Mary, for instance, be asked to serve in that area under him. The governor also reported that he had already "intimated to him" that he would like him to look in on the meetings of the Portland Parochial Board whenever important matters were on the agenda for discussion. See Co137/343, dispatch 1715/2/1857, Darling to Lytton. Microfilm, West Indies Collection, University of the West Indies, Mona, Jamaica.

10. Crop accounts 1B/11/4/81/15, Jamaica Archives.
11. Thomas C. Holt, *The Problem of Freedom* (Kingston: Ian Randle Publishers, 1992), 63.
12. Hall, *Free Jamaica*, 110fn.
13. CO 137/212, dispatch 522, July to August 1836, stipendiary magistrate's reports Sligo to Glenelg. Microfilm, West Indies Collection, University of the West Indies, Mona, Jamaica.
14. CO 137/212, dispatch 203.
15. CO 137/212, dispatch 203.
16. CO 137/212, dispatch 401.
17. Crop accounts 1B/11/4/81/15, Jamaica Archives.
18. CO 137/212, 106 in dispatch 537, Sligo to Glenelg, June 1836.
19. Smithin Wilmot's presentation "St Mary/Woodside Area: A General History to the Woodside Community", in January 1995, drew my attention to Woodside as a coffee-producing area.
20. Ibid.
21. Appendix to the seventh report from the Select Committee on Sugar and Coffee Planting, Great Britain Parliament House of Commons (1848), 229.
22. Wright, *Lady Nugent's Journal*, 78.
23. *Jamaica Almanack*, 1840.
24. Ibid.
25. Vestry proceedings (parish of St Mary), 1847–1850, Jamaica Archives.
26. StM 94, Map Collection, National Library of Jamaica, Kingston. All other map collections mentioned in this chapter are found at the National Library.
27. StM 154.
28. StM 558.

29. Deeds LOS 487, folio no. 169, Island Records Office, Twickenham Park, Jamaica. All other deeds mentioned in this chapter are found in this office.
30. *Jamaica Almanack,* 1832.
31. Ibid., 1840.
32. Sold to William Sutherland/Litherland Stm1227.
33. StM 586. This and other maps mentioned in this chapter are from the collection cited at note 18.
34. StM 51 – land sold to small settlers in 1843.
35. Conversations with Mrs Pearl Crossman of Woodside, 1994.
36. Patterson, *Sociology of Slavery,* 81.
37. Deeds LOS 687, folio no. 164.
38. Conversations with Mr Arnold Remikie, 1996. This name has a variety of spellings – Remekie, Remique, Rennieki – the earliest of which the family being aware is Ramiki, which appeared sometimes as Raniki.
39. Patterson, *Sociology of Slavery,* 80. Information in the rest of the paragraph comes from this source.
40. Register of Baptisms, Marriages and Burials (St Mary), 1826–57, Jamaica Archives. The Reverend Archer whom we see as the official clergyman in several baptisms, is listed as the father of Lucy-Ann of Rock Spring, baptized in 1841. In this collection are found the registers of baptism, marriage and burials mentioned in this chapter.
41. Higman, *Jamaica Surveyed,* 270. Also see Brathwaite, *The Development of Creole Society,* appendix III.
42. *Talk, Talk: An Ashanti Tale* retold by Deborah M. Newton Chocolate (Mahwah, N.J.: Troll Associates, 1993) is very much a tale told by Sandy Davis at community gatherings at Woodside. He learned this tale in Hopewell, a part of greater Woodside. There are people in the area who know how to cook foo-foo, the popular West African meal.
43. I experienced this annual five-day festival in Akropong in Ghana in 1994.
44. Some of these sounds have been caught in the interview done by Laura Lomas with John Fyffe, 24 July 1993, and on video by Gettysburg College students in 1995. The *manalva* is done now only as theatre.
45. Register of Slave Returns (St Mary) 1B/11/7/92, Jamaica Archives.
46. See Edward (Kamau) Brathwaite, *Wars of Respect* (Kingston: Agency for Public Information, 1977), 21, and especially Shirley Gordon, *God Almighty Make We Free* (Bloomington: Indiana University Press, 1996), 42.
47. In *Savacou,* no. 5 (June 1971): 27.
48. Register of Slave Returns (St Mary) 1B/11/7/42, 58 and 92. Mary Gibb belongs to a long list of St Mary slave holders who do so and are likely to be Quakers. Frances Neilson, William John's mother, is not one of them. Margaret Buchanan Neilson, James Neilson and of course William John, do

so. Others are Timberlake, Oldacre, Northover, Shand, Shreyer, Patterson,
Larchin Gordon and some smallholders who are women and illiterate.

49. Register of Slave Returns 1B/11/7/5 and 6, 74, Jamaica Archives.

50. See Martha Beckwith, *Black Roadways* (New York: Negro University Press, 1969). "Long Bubby Susan" is the heading of a chapter. Today the carving is called One Bubby Susan but Mrs Vie Campbell, *née* Hermitt, remembers calling it Long Bubby Susan and that there was an African-sounding phrase that one said when speaking of this "image". She can only remember a part of it: "Ef yu no gi one waki."

51. Contributed by Mrs Pearl Crossman of Rock Spring.

52. Beckwith, *Black Roadways*.

53. Brathwaite, *Wars of Respect*.

54. *Baptist Missionary Herald,* March 1838. Collection of Baptist Church Library, Half-Way Tree, Kingston, Jamaica.

55. *Baptist Missionary Herald,* 1827.

56. *Baptist Missionary Herald,* February 1835.

57. Mrs Gladys Walker's history of the church written from oral sources appears in *The Banana Church,* a pamphlet prepared for the seventy-fifth anniversary of the churches in the Highgate cure in 1972.

58. Register of Baptisms, Marriages and Burials 1826–1857.

59. Interview with Gilbert Walker in 1993 done by Bob Fredrickson, student at Gettysburg College.

60. StM 586.

61. Ibid.

62. StM 51.

63. "Marriages of white persons and persons of pale condition", in Register of Baptisms, Marriages and Burials 1826–1857.

64. References to the deaths in this paragraph are found in the registers above as well as in some cases in the general register of births, deaths, marriages housed in the Armoury, Records Office, Spanish Town, Jamaica. This was found in the general registry of deaths, folio no. 250 (1832).

65. "Marriages of white persons".

66. General Register of Deaths, folio no. 252 (?).

67. Ibid.

68. Ibid.

69. Register at the Armoury and Register of Slave Returns (St Mary) 1B/11/7/42, 58 and 92, folio no. 431 (1843).

70. Ibid., folio 429 (1832).

71. *Jamaica Almanack,* 1832.

72. Register of Slave Returns (St Mary) 1B/11/7/42, 58 and 92, folio no. 432 (1832).

73. Ibid.
74. "Burial of Whites" in Register of Baptisms, Marriages and Burials (St Mary) 1817–1825, and Register of Slave Returns (St Mary) 1B/11/7/92, Jamaica Archives.
75. *Baptist Missionary Herald,* June 1845, 93. Baptist Church Archives, Kingston, Jamaica.
76. Ibid., October 1840.
77. Ibid., March 1841.
78. Ibid., April 1841.
79. Swithin Wilmot, "The Meaning of Slavery: Blacks and Whites and Labour Struggle in Jamaica, 1838–1865" (paper presented at the conference Slavery, Emancipation and the Shaping of the Caribbean Society, 8–10 December 1988, St Augustine, Trinidad), 5.
80. Swithin Wilmot at Ernest Brodber Memorial Lecture, b l a c k s p a c e, Woodside, April 1989.
81. CO 137/261 Metcalfe to Stanley 1842, encl. Report from the C'ttee to whom was referred the petition of the freeholder and inhabitants of the western part of the parish of St George and the eastern part of St Mary, Jamaica Archives.

Chapter 6

1. Register of Baptisms, Marriages and Burials 1826–1857 and Baptisms, Marriages and Burials 1871–1887, Jamaica Archives, Spanish Town (St Mary and St Thomas-in-the-Vale are the references for the marriages in this chapter).
2. Lomas, interview with John Fyffe. Re-interviewed by the author.
3. Register of Property Tax from 1 August 1869 to 31 July 1870 and Parish Council of St Mary – statement of land tax and arrears paid in St Mary 1881–1882, Jamaica Archives.
4. Register of Births, Deaths and Marriages 1842, Armoury, Island Records Office, Spanish Town, Jamaica.
5. Crop accounts 1B/11/94/82/144 (1839), Jamaica Archives.
6. StM 156, Map Collection, National Library of Jamaica, Kingston. All other maps mentioned in this chapter are found at the National Library.
7. Group interview of Woodside community, January 1994.
8. Register as at note 1.
9. Patterson, *Sociology of Slavery,* 83. This source states that the offering was less than one acre to ten slaves.
10. Interviews with Mrs Leah Ferguson-Brissett and Mr Levi Hudson.
11. StM 558.

12. See Hall, *Free Jamaica,* 186–90, for further information.
13. Talks with Mrs Leah Ferguson-Brissett, 1995.
14. The issue is identified by Mrs Brissett above as Mrs Margaret Reid, a brown woman who lived in Rock Spring.
15. *Jamaica Almanack,* 1811–40.
16. Ibid., 1832.
17. See Register of Slave Returns (St Mary) for 1829, filed under Neilson 1B/11/7/113, Jamaica Archives.
18. Ibid.
19. Talks with Mrs Leah Ferguson-Brissett, 1995.
20. Interviews with Eustace Brown, 1995, and his son Everald Brown, 1996.
21. Interview with Busha Brown, 1995.
22. Diagrams dated 5 November 1890, 3 March 1898 and 6 May 1908, in the private collection of Everald Brown. Also the 1941 will of Charles Thaddeus Brown.
23. Verene Shepherd, *Transients to Settlers: The Experience of Indians in Jamaica* (Leeds: Peepal Tree Press, 1994), 53.
24. Hall, *Free Jamaica,* 109–11.
25. Lomas, interview with John Fyffe. Re-interviewed by the author.
26. Register of Slave Returns (St Mary) for 1829, filed under Neilson 1B/11/7/113, Jamaica Archives.
27. Lomas, interview with John Fyffe.
28. Interview with Eustace Brown, 1995.
29. Group interview of Woodside community, January 1994. It is also said that the plaque in the Woodside church honouring Elizabeth Grant (*née* Brown) is placed where her bed was in that former great house.
30. Register of Slave Returns (St Mary) for 1829, filed under Neilson 1B/11/7/113, Jamaica Archives.
31. Diagrams dated 5 November 1890, 3 March 1898 and 6 May 1908, in the private collection of Everald Brown. Also the 1941 will of Charles Thaddeus Brown.
32. Deeds 487, folio no. 169, Island Records Office, Twickenham Park, Jamaica.
33. *Jamaica Almanack,* 1811–1840
34. Register of Slave Returns (St Mary) 1826, filed under Neilson 1B/11/7/92 and for 1829, 1B/11/7/113, Jamaica Archives.
35. Register of Slave Returns (St Mary) 1817, filed under Hermit 1B/11/7/5, Jamaica Archives.
36. Correspondence and talks with Mrs Vie Campbell, *née* Hermitt, 1996.
37. Title issued in 1902, in the possession of Mr Arnold Remikie of Rock Spring.
38. Interview with Eustace Brown, 1995.
39. StM 599.

40. Talks with Mrs John Hermitt, 1995.
41. Interview with Eustace Brown, 1995.
42. Ibid.
43. Hall, *Free Jamaica,* 109–11.
44. Register of Slave Returns (St Mary) for 1829, filed under Neilson 1B/11/7/113, Jamaica Archives.
45. Plaque in the Anglican church.
46. Conveyance document dated 1898 in the possession of Everald Brown.
47. *Jamaica Almanack,* 1811–40. Timberlakes were also property owners. Timberlake is also a slave name. See Register of Baptisms cited in note 1.
48. StM 688.
49. *Handbook of Jamaica,* 1842.
50. Hall, *Free Jamaica,* 22.
51. Appendix no. 7, votes of the House Assembly of Jamaica, 1842. John Maxwell, subagent to John Ewart, agent general of immigrants for St Thomas-in-the-Vale, 30 September 1842. Jamaica Archives.
52. CO 137/272, Elgin to Stanley, encl. 3 in dispatch 9, 29 February 1843. Microfilm, West Indies Collection, University of the West Indies, Mona, Jamaica.
53. Interview with Mr Arnold Remikie by Marie Voley, student at Gettysburg College, 1994.
54. Talks with Teacher Thompson of Woodside School, 1996.
55. Talks with Mrs Gladys Walker in my youth.
56. Talks with Mrs Leah Ferguson-Brissett, 1995.
57. Register of Slave Returns (St Mary) 1823, filed under Neilson 1B/11/7/58, Jamaica Archives.
58. Interview with Mr Keith Williams by Torey Williams, student at Gettysburg College, 1994.

Chapter 7

1. *Baptist Missionary Herald,* March 1841.
2. Laws of Jamaica XLIII, 12 December 1833.
3. Register of Baptisms, Marriages and Burials (St Mary) 1826–1857, Jamaica Archives, Spanish Town.
4. Ibid.
5. The evidence of the foundation stone of the church at Richmond Hill.
6. Handbook of the Parish of St Mary, 1841–1842, National Library of Jamaica.
7. Register of Baptisms, Marriages and Burials (St Mary) 1826–1857, Register of Burials (St Mary) 1871–1881, vol. 17, Jamaica Archives, Spanish Town.

8. *Journal of the Synod of the Church of England in Jamaica*, 1883, 1887. Hereafter cited as *Journal of the Synod*.

9. Register of Baptisms, Marriages and Burials (St Mary) 1826–1857, Jamaica Archives, Spanish Town.

10. Report on Woodside by Mrs Gladys Walker in *The Banana Church* (1972), 35.

11. *Baptist Missionary Herald*, February 1831, 14.

12. *Journal of the Synod*, 1876.

13. Ibid., 1876, 1898, 1893. Figures for the succeeding paragraph are also from this source.

14. Register of Property Tax 1/8/1869–31/7/1870. Statement of Land Tax and areas paid in St Mary 1881–1882, Jamaica Archives.

15. Brathwaite, *The Development of Creole Society*, 165.

16. As I witnessed in Aquapem, Ghana in 1994.

17. Beckwith, *Black Roadways*, 147.

18. Talks with Arnold Remikie, 1996.

19. Interview with Remikie by Marie Voley and follow-up talks with the author.

20. *Journal of the Synod*, 1876, 1907, 1911, 1928, 1929 are the sources of data for this paragraph.

21. Report on Woodside in *The Banana Church*, 35.

22. *Journal of the Synod*, 1876, 1898, 1907, 1911, 1925, 1928, 1929 are sources of data for this and the succeeding paragraphs.

23. Ibid.

24. Interview with Mr Vernal Kelly, 1989.

25. *Journal of the Synod*, 1895.

26. *Handbook of Jamaica*, 1882.

27. Veront M. Satchell, *From Plots to Plantation* (Kingston: Institute of Social and Economic Research, University of the West Indies, 1990), 133.

28. Talks with N.F. Walker, 1993–96.

29. Indenture between David Renichie and James Gayleard, 1854, in the possession of Arnold Remikie.

30. Identified through Register of Births and Parish Returns (St Mary) 1841–1842, Jamaica Archives.

31. Several oral reports of Woodside citizens.

32. Interview with Renford Toomer by Jennifer MacDonald, student at Randolph Macon College, 7 January 1994.

33. *The Banana Church*, 25.

34. Erna Brodber, *Perceptions of Caribbean Women* (Kingston: Institute of Social and Economic Research [Eastern Caribbean], University of the West Indies, 1982), 28.

35. Howard Johnson, "The Anti-Chinese Riots of 1918 in Jamaica", *Immigrants and Minorities* 2, no. 1 (March 1983).

36. Ibid., 59.
37. Register of Property Tax, Jamaica Archives.
38. Ibid.
39. *Jamaica Almanack,* 1824 and StM 583 (1806).
40. Interview with Mr Roy Crossman by Kristine Svec, student at Gettysburg College, 1994.
41. Register of Property Tax 1/8/1869–31/7/1870.
42. Ibid.
43. Interview with Nyah Morrison, 1995.
44. Register of Property Tax 1/8/1869–31/7/1870.
45. StM 583, Map Collection, National Library of Jamaica.
46. Talks with Mr Levi Hudson, 1996.
47. Group interview with Woodside residents, January 1994.
48. Ibid.
49. Interview with Mr Vernal Kelly, 1989.
50. The relevant St Mary map found in the map collection of the National Library of Jamaica. The Library is not certain whether the map was produced in 1651 or 1731.
51. Register of Property Tax, Jamaica Archives.
52. Handbook of the Parish of St Mary, 1841–1842, is the source of data for the rest of the paragraph. Note too that Pear Tree Grove, St Mary was at this time the address of Pupley the immigration agent. See CO 137/273 encl. 3 in dispatch 9, Elgin to Stanley, February 1843.
53. CO 137/273.
54. Deeds 487, folio 169, Island Records Office, Twickenham Park, Jamaica.
55. His name appears in *Jamaica Almanack,* 1811–1838 as at some time an assistant judge and captain in the militia.
56. Wills LOS 109, folio no. 112 and 110, folio no. 103. Island Records Office.
57. According to the Registry of Church Properties in the Anglican Office, fifteen acres and one rood, a part of Woodside, was conveyed to the Incorporated lay body by J. Neilson et al. The conveyance was on 14 October 1881 and the date of transfer was 2 November 1881. The certificate of title is N5 11/Folio 217. Thanks to Mr Melbourne Wint for contributing this piece of datum.

Afterword

1. Swithin Wilmot at Ernest Brodber Memorial Lecture, b l a c k s p a c e, Woodside, April 1989.
2. William Kelly was a slave on the Woodside plantation between 1817 and

1831. Another William, this time of Carron Hall, was baptized in 1850 at Woodside, according to the Register of Baptisms, Marriages and Deaths (St Mary) 1826–1857. Chances are these are Mr Kelly's kin.

3. *Handbook of Jamaica,* 1912.

4. Mervyn Alleyne, *Roots of Jamaican Culture* (London: Pluto Press, 1998), 93; also talks with Roy Crossman, 1995.

5. Talks with Mrs Pearl Crossman of Rock Spring, 1995–96.

6. A myth I heard while I collected material for fieldwork here towards an MSc thesis, University of the West Indies, 1968. The myth was voiced once more in a community session here in Woodside in 1996.

7. Holt, *The Problem of Freedom,* 61–64.

8. The opinion of Mr Arnold Remikie/Remique/Ranniki/Ramiki who could be from new African stock and whose forebears were landowners in the area since 1854.

9. I remember hearing my aunt, a "foreign" wife born and raised twelve miles away, talking about the negative response to her.

10. Interviews with Roland Forbes, 1994, and Eustace Brown, 1996.

Bibliography

Archival Sources

ISLAND RECORDS OFFICE, TWICKENHAM PARK, JAMAICA
Deeds
Wills

JAMAICA ARCHIVES, SPANISH TOWN

Vestry Proceedings (parish of St Mary) 1847–1850
Crop accounts
Register of Slave Returns
Register of Baptisms, Marriages and Burials for St Mary and St Thomas-in-the-
    Vale
Register of Property Tax for St Mary
General Register of Births, Deaths and Marriages
Jamaica – Minutes of the Council
Report of the Great Britain House of Commons, Select Committee of on Sugar
    and Coffee Planting 1848
Appendix of the House of Assembly, Jamaica 1842

NATIONAL LIBRARY OF JAMAICA, KINGSTON
Map Collection for St Mary
Parish Returns for St Mary

WEST INDIES COLLECTION, UNIVERSITY OF THE WEST INDIES,
MONA, JAMAICA
Governor's dispatches (Jamaica) CO 137/209–265 and 343. Microfilm.

Private Collections

Everald Brown – conveyances
Arnold Remikie – titles

Jacob Lee – conveyance
Bishie (Noel Walker) – titles and conveyances

Oral Sources

Bishie (Noel) Walker
Roland Forbes
Leonard Hermitt
Vie Campbell, *née* Hermitt
E. Burrowes, *née* Hermitt
Mrs John Hermitt
Mrs Leah Ferguson-Brisset
Eustace Brown
John Fyffe
Roy Crossman
Keith Williams
Ronald Toomer
Pearl Crossman
Gilbert Walker
Vernal Kelly
Arnold Remikie
Levi Hudson

Group interviews with members of the Woodside community

Gravestones and Plaques

John Neilson (now stolen)
William Turner
Edward Burrowes
James and Elizabeth Grant

Publications

PERIODICALS

Baptist Missionary Herald
Handbook of Jamaica
Jamaica Almanack
Journal of the Synod of the Church of England in Jamaica

Books and Articles

Alleyne, Mervyn. *Roots of Jamaican Culture*. London: Pluto Press, 1998.

Beckwith, Martha. *Black Roadways*. New York: Negro Universities Press, 1969.

Brathwaite, Edward [Kamau]. *The Development of Creole Society in Jamaica 1770–1820*. Oxford: Clarendon Press, 1971.

———. *Wars of Respect*. Kingston: Agency for Public Information, 1977.

Brodber, Erna. "Life in Jamaica in the Early Twentieth Century: A Presentation of Ninety Oral Accounts". Typescript, Institute of Social and Economic Research Documentation Centre, University of the West Indies, Jamaica, 1980.

———. *Perceptions of Caribbean Women*. Kingston: Institute of Social and Economic Research (Eastern Caribbean), University of the West Indies, 1982.

Cassidy, F.G., and R.B. Le Page, eds. *Dictionary of Jamaican English*, 2nd ed. Kingston: University of the West Indies Press, 2002.

Chevannes, Barry. "Revival and Black Struggle". *Savacou*, no. 5 (June 1971).

Gordon, Shirley. *God Almighty Make We Free*. Bloomington: Indiana University Press, 1996.

Hall, Douglas. *Free Jamaica*. New Haven: Yale University Press, 1959.

Heuman, Gad. *Between Black and White*. Westport: Greenwood Press, 1981.

Higman, B.W. *Jamaica Surveyed*. Kingston: Institute of Jamaica Publications, 1988.

Holt, Thomas C. *The Problem of Freedom*. Kingston: Ian Randle Publishers, 1992.

Johnson, Howard. "The Anti-Chinese Riots of 1918 in Jamaica". *Immigrants and Minorities* 2, no. 1 (March 1983).

Kopytoff, Ivor, and Suzanne Miers. *Slavery in Africa*. Madison: University of Wisconsin Press, 1977.

Mathurin, Lucille. "A Historical Study of Women in Jamaica from 1655–1844". PhD diss., University of the West Indies, Mona, Jamaica, 1974.

Newton Chocolate, Deborah M. *Talk, Talk: An Ashanti Tale*. Mahwah, N.J.: Troll Associates, 1993.

Patterson, Orlando. *Sociology of Slavery*. Kingston, Jamaica: Sangster's Book Stores, 1967.

Satchell, Veront M. *From Plots to Plantation*. Kingston: Institute of Social and Economic Research, University of the West Indies, 1990.

Shepherd, Verene. *Transients to Settlers: the Experience of Indians in Jamaica*. Leeds: Peepal Tree Press, 1994.

Walker, Gladys. "History of Woodside". In *The Banana Church*. Pamphlet for the seventy-fifth anniversary of the churches in the Highgate cure, 1972

Williams, R.L. *The Coffee Industry of Jamaica*. Kingston, Jamaica: Institute of Social and Economic Research, University of the West Indies, 1975.

Wright, Phillip, ed. *Lady Nugent's Journal of Her Residence in Jamaica from 1801 to 1805*. Kingston: Institute of Jamaica, 1966.

Index

Note: Family names in parentheses show alternative spellings. Names in square brackets indicate the person's slave name before baptism.

Abolition Act (1834), 33, 79, 82–83. *See also* apprenticeship
Abrahams, Isabella, 104
Africa
    cultural influence of, 57, 64–65, 73–74, 126–27, 144–45, 147
    migrants from, 120–21, 125, 130–31
Agorsah, Kofi, 12
agriculture. *See also specific crops;*
    farmers; plantations
      diversification of, 135–36
      and marketing, 132, 142
      militia and, 38
      in Woodside, 50, 131–32, 134
Aitkin family, 130, 148
Aitkin, Mary, 120
Aitkin Town, 120, 148
Alexander, Abraham, 70
Anderson family, 129, 133
Anderson, Joseph, 44
Andrews, Oaxley, 11
Andrews, William, 46, 47
Anglican Church
    in Woodside, 124, 130, 140, 144
      baptisms in, 53, 65, 90, 94, 124–26
      and Baptists, 47, 93–94, 101–2, 123–24, 125
    and blacks, 47, 103, 148
    expansion of, 97–98, 127–29
    and immigrants, 132, 133
    records of, 96–98
    state support of, 102, 123–24
Antonio (slave man), 81
apprenticeship, 79, 82–86, 116. *See also* slaves
Arawaks (Tainos), 5, 92
Archer, James Walter, 45, 90, 93, 95, 100, 124
    and A.G. Fyfe, 45, 103
Archibald, Elise, 111, 119
assemblymen, 40

bananas, 131–32, 135–36
baptism, 97–98
    of adults, 125
    in Anglican Church, 53, 65, 90, 94, 124–26
    decline in, 127–28
    names given at, 65–71, 90
    of slaves, 65, 70–71
Baptist Church, 30
    African, 94
    American, 91–92
    clergy of, 49, 123

treatment of, 75–77, 78, 79, 80
and whites, 53–55, 78
women as, 55, 147
Smailfield, 11, 48, 85, 111
   as coffee plantation, 17, 23, 48, 134
   crops grown at, 23, 48, 134, 135–36
   extent of, 14, 21–24
   families at, 98, 104, 106, 108–9, 111
   land ownership at, 21–24, 28, 37, 40, 51, 87, 119
   tombstone at, 7–10
Smith family, 96
Smith, James, 85
Society of Friends, 55
Spaniards, 5
Springfield, 46
Spring Valley, 110, 112–13. *See also* Pear Tree Grove
Stanbury family, 96, 128, 132, 133
Stanbury, E., 106
Stanbury, George, 105
Stanbury, James, 70
Stapleton, 11, 15–17, 69
   families at, 96, 97, 98, 106–8, 111, 120
   land ownership at, 27–28, 119
Stephens, John, 98
Sterling Castle. *See* Stirling Castle
Stevens, Elizabeth, 111, 119
Stevens, John, 26, 85
Stevenson, Nicholas, 98
Stewart family, 96, 107, 129, 134
Stewart, Charles, 111
Stewart, Peggy, 107, 112, 119
Stewart Town, 79
stipendiary magistrates, 40, 84–86, 100, 102–3, 116, 130
Stirling Castle, 78, 114
Stony Hill, 35
sugar plantations, 7, 12, 17, 50
   failure of, 21, 86, 131

slaves on, 89
small, 134, 136, 142
women on, 49
Sunday schools, 125–26, 127
surveyors, 72. *See also* Neilson, William
Symmonds, Rosetta, 98. *See also* Simmonds family

Tainos (Arawaks), 5
tata, 74, 118
taxes, 11, 101, 112, 114, 118–19, 121–22, 129, 145. *See also* Vestry
   Anglican Church and, 102, 123
   records of, 105–10
Taylor, Richard, 98
Taylor, Simon (black), 94
Taylor, Simon (uncle), 15, 52
Taylor, Sir Simon (nephew), 52
teachers, 128, 148
Thaw (Thor) family, 31, 98
Thaw (Thor), Oxford, 98
Thomas family, 109, 111, 128
Thomas, Blanche, 106, 119
Thomas, Gracey Ann, 98
Thomas, I.P., 134
Thomas, John, 134, 135
Thomas, Letitia, 70, 98
Thomas, Martha, 111, 119
Thomas, Richard, 21, 24, 85, 87, 109
Thomas, Robert, 87, 109
Thomas, William, 95, 106, 108, 134
Thompson family, 106–7
Thompson, Diana, 98, 125
Thor. *See* Thaw
Timberlake family, 96, 120
Timberlake, Elizabeth, 50, 79, 100
Timberlake, Mitchell, 97
Timberlake, William, 79
tombstones, 7–10, 14
Toomer, Nathan, 132
Top Yard, 118
traders, 89, 90. *See also* shopkeepers
tradesmen, 44, 88, 118